MODERN ENGLISH ESSAYS

SAXON SERIES IN ENGLISH AS A SECOND LANGUAGE

Grant Taylor, Consulting Editor

Advanced English Exercises

American English Reader

Index to Modern English

Learning American English

Mastering American English

Mastering Spoken English (Tapes-Records)

Mastering Spoken English Workbook

Modern English Essays

Modern English Workbook

Modern Spoken English

Practicing American English

Reading American History

MODERN ENGLISH ESSAYS

Thomas Lee Crowell, Jr.
Late Professor of English
Columbia University and Hunter College

McGRAW-HILL COMPANY OF CANADA LIMITED

TORONTO New York London Sydney Johannesburg Mexico Panama

MODERN ENGLISH ESSAYS

Library of Congress Catalog Card Number   63-22505

14733

1 2 3 4 5 6 7 8 9 0   McB-68   7 6 5 4 3 2 1 0 9 8

Printed and bound in Canada

PREFACE

The essays in this book are for advanced students of English as a second language. They are representative of the reading that is done by college students or by students preparing for college. The authors of the essays, who are accomplished writers, are members of academic institutions such as Hunter College, Columbia University, New York University, Brooklyn College, Colgate University, and the University of Michigan.

The subject matter, which is of lasting interest and value, ranges from cooking to philosophy and includes personal reminiscences as well as articles on history, biography, mythology, sociology, literature, and science. The content of the reading, in other words, is wide-ranging; a glance through the Table of Contents suggests the multiplicity of ideas touched upon.

The major problems of an advanced student are reading comprehension and accurate expression of his thoughts. He wants and is expected to read a great deal rapidly, to understand what he reads, and to be able to express himself fluently in speech and writing. His difficulties do not ordinarily stem from lack of acquaintance with ideas; most often, they arise from his limited experience with the manner of expressing ideas in another language. His need, therefore, is to broaden his acquaintance with literate expression in that language.

How does literate expression differ from other kinds of expression? One of the outstanding ways in which it differs is the frequency of occurrence of words. As the exercises in this book demonstrate, the words used in writing are virtually the same as those used in ordinary conversation, but their frequency of use is different. Certain words are often spoken but less often written; other words are used frequently in writing but seldom in conversation. To become fully acquainted with the literate vocabulary, therefore, one must read and use the words of his reading. This book contains a broad sampling of the literate vocabulary and provides numerous exercises to aid the student in making it his own.

Another way in which literate expression differs is in density of expression. Good writing and speech tend to be succinct, to say much in a few words. For example, certain syntactical constructions—such as dependent clauses, modifying phrases, and appositives—are used more frequently by educated than by uneducated persons. Furthermore, rhetorical devices such as metaphor and irony, though employed by all sorts of persons, often distinguish the literate from the illiterate. The student needs to become conversant with those methods of expression in order to increase his comprehension, both visual and aural, and to improve his own expression. This book offers intensive practice in those means of expression.

One of the aims of the book is to demonstrate the scope and flexibility of literate expression. An article on astronomy, for example, employs words and syntactical patterns that appear in a piece of writing on money or food or Shakespeare or the perfectability of the human condition. There is, to be sure, such a thing as specialized vocabulary—the words used with special application in some particular field of endeavor. Nevertheless, that vocabulary does not occur in isolation: it is conveyed by the vehicle, the total mechanism of the English language. In addition, much that seems at first glance to be specialized is not limited in use—for instance, psychiatric locutions appear in literary criticism; economic and sports terms also serve in music and politics. It is highly important for the student to know that the words and constructions of literate expression occur in college lectures and readings and in the conversations of literate people.

How does the language ability of a literate person differ from that of an uneducated one? It differs primarily in range. Not only is the educated man able to express himself well actively—that is, in speaking and writing—but he has also developed his passive skills; he understands what is spoken and written.

The purpose of this book, then, is to increase the student's four faculties in the English language: the passive faculties of reading and listening efficiently and the active faculties of writing and speaking effectively.

I wish to express my appreciation to the sixteen authors of the essays for their generous and good contributions. I also gratefully acknowledge the kind and wise comments of the numerous students and teachers who used the material of the book in its trial stages. I am particularly indebted for assistance received from Howard P. Linton, Robert Parslow, and Grant Taylor.

Thomas Lee Crowell, Jr.

SUGGESTIONS FOR USE

Learning in context and through practice is the governing principle throughout this book. Bits of the English language are not viewed in isolation; they are treated as parts of a whole. The meaningful utterance is considered to be the minimum unit. Repetition is the device employed to facilitate the acquisition of knowledge and of the skills needed to utilize that knowledge.

The essays are grouped in units of five. In each unit the second essay, along with its exercises, serves as a reinforcement of the words, phrases, and patterns in the first essay and its exercises, and the fourth essay serves as a reinforcement of the third. The fifth essay has the nature of a review of the material in the preceding four essays. Although the five essays are interrelated, each is also a separate entity and can be used without reference to the other four.

To illustrate the ways in which the book may be used, the following paragraphs give a fairly detailed discussion of Essay 1, Essay 2, and the first thirteen exercises.

First, ESSAY 1 can be read aloud to the students. Since initial aural impressions are the strongest, it is advisable to have the first oral reading done as expertly as possible. The entire selection can be read while the students look at the essay in their books. If facilities are available, the first reading can be done in the language laboratory to save class time. The essay is read without interruptions for explanations or questions: Interruptions break the continuity of thought and expression and lessen the pleasure of listening. The reader speaks in the customary lecturing fashion, a little more slowly than in conversation but not so slowly as to destroy the rhythm of the sentence. He stresses only the normally stressed syllables and is particularly careful not to stress the articles *a, an,* and *the.* He pauses only between phrases and sentences.

With EXERCISE 1, which lists the plurisyllabic words in the essay according to the place of stress, many teachers prefer to pronounce each word aloud first. They intentionally exaggerate the length, loudness and pitch of the stressed syllable. The students repeat each word immediately, either in chorus or in rotation. If there is time, the teacher repeats each word after the students. Exercise 1 is also adaptable for laboratory work.

One of the most important features of English is word stress, but it is also one of the most troublesome, since there are few guides to the place of stress. However, the teacher can profitably discuss the regularities and refer to them whenever an example occurs. For instance, words ending in *–cial, –cially, –cian, –cience, –ciency, –cient, –ciently, –cion, –cious, –ciously, –sian, –sion, –sional, –sionally, –tial, –tially, –tian, –tience, –tient, –tiently, –tion, –tional, –tionally, –tious,* and *–tiously* regularly have their stress on the vowel preceding those endings. The essays have nineteen words beginning with the letter *a* alone which illustrate this point—for example, *action, ancient,* and *auspicious.* Furthermore, the teacher can point out that in such words the *–ci–. –si–,* and *–ti–* are regularly pronounced like *sh* in *shoe,* except that *–ti–* preceded by an *s* is pronounced like *ch* in *church* (e.g., *question*) and that *–si–* is voiced when preceded by a vowel (e.g., *occasion*).

Incidentally, a few plurisyllabic words are not included in the exercise because they may be stressed either of two ways in the context; for example, *translate, resource, narrate,* and *detail* may have the primary stress on either the first or second syllable without change of meaning. However, if a word has only one customary stress pattern in a particular context, it is listed. For example, when used as verbs, *conduct* and *subject* will be listed as having the stress on the second syllable; used as nouns, they will be listed with the stress on the first.

EXERCISE 2 asks the students to read the essay aloud after they have heard it read aloud and after they have had practice in stressing the plurisyllabic words. Thus, if it is necessary for the teacher to correct pronunciation or rhythm, the students know the reason. The method of distributing the reading may vary: One student may read the entire essay, a paragraph, or a sentence. The teacher can drill the students on phrasing: not stopping between the parts of a breath group emphasizing only stressed syllables in a group, and not emphasizing customarily unstressed words like articles, prepositions, and conjunctions. He can drill on intonation: keeping the pitch of the voice at a middle level for any pause other than the one at the end of a sentence, lowering the pitch at the end of most sentences, but letting the pitch remain high at the end of questions which do not begin with the *wh* words *who, whom, whose, which, what, why, when, where,* and *how.*

EXERCISE 3 has the primary purpose of making sure that the students have understood the content of the essay. The questions are paraphrases of the ideas in the essay. Since at times a misinterpretation of a part of the essay may be cleared up by the questions, the students should study the latter very carefully. The questions may be asked in class by either the teacher or the students and answered by the students. If class time is limited, the teacher may select questions which will reveal whether the students have understood certain lines of the essay. For written tests, the students may be directed to give the answers to all or some of the questions.

Exercise 3 has another very important purpose (as does Exercise 8) — that of developing the students' ability in conversation. To accomplish this, the following procedure may be used. Preferably, the questions are taken up on a day after the essay has been read and Exercises 1 and 2 have been finished. The students keep their books closed, and the questions are asked with normal conversational delivery. At first, the students may have difficulty in understanding the spoken questions even though they have studied the written form. However, patience and persistence will be rewarded: Very soon they will be able to understand and respond with ease.

The questions in both Exercise 3 and Exercise 8 have purposely been constructed to call for a brief response, usually only one or two words or the short-answer pattern of "Yes, I do" or "No, it wasn't," in which nearly all students need much drill. It is suggested that students not be required to give full-sentence oral answers to the questions, since that type of response is very unusual in normal conversation. For writing practice either in class or at home, students may give full-sentence answers. The patterns of the questions have also been deliberately varied so as to widen the students' acquaintance with question types.

EXERCISE 4, by having the students summarize the essay, offers them the opportunity to use orally the words and patterns that occur in the essay and the preceding exercises. EXERCISE 5 provides the same opportunity for written expression. In the two exercises the students may give either paraphrases or a near repetition of the essay. Both types of summarizing provide valuable practice.

After the students have heard and read the essay and have become thoroughly familiar with the writing, they are ready for exact duplication of it. EXERCISE 6, then, calls for dictation.

Here is a procedure which many teachers use. Having selected five sentences from the essay, the teacher gives the students the following instructions. He tells them to write on alternate lines so that he will have space to correct their mistakes. Then he tells them that from the moment he begins until he takes up their papers, they must not say a word: They cannot ask him to repeat. Since every sentence will be said four times, they should be able to grasp a word later if they do not understand it the first time. Next, he tells them to listen—not begin to write—when he says a sentence the first time so that they can comprehend the meaning of the whole sentence.

The teacher says the first sentence in as conversational a way as possible, with ordinary phrasing and intonation. Then he repeats it in phrases, pausing after each phrase long enough to allow the students to write the words. For instance, he says, "I pitied him . . . and went out of my way . . . to help him . . . get adjusted to his work . . . and to make him . . . feel at home." He never says the words singly, and he never, for example, isolates *a* or *the* or abnormally stresses personal pronouns and adjectives. Also, the students should have sufficient time to write but not excessive time: They need practice in writing rapidly.

The teacher says the sentence a third time so that the students can look at what they have written. He proceeds to the second sentence, says it normally, repeats it in phrases while the students write, and then says it again as a normal sentence. He continues in this manner until he has finished all the sentences. Finally, he goes back and says each sentence, one after the other, for the fourth time while the students check their writing. He collects the papers and then so that the students may immediately see the exact form, asks them to open their books and read aloud the passages that have just been dictated. He takes the papers home, marks out misspellings, writes in corrections, scores the papers, and returns them at the next meeting. He counts off not only for misspellings but also, for instance, for *a*'s and *the*'s omitted, incorrectly inserted, or confused, and for missing final *s*'s and *ed*'s. If students make more than a certain number of errors, they are asked to rewrite the entire dictation. At the meeting in which the teacher returns the papers, he again reads the sentences aloud while the students look at their corrected papers. Then he asks students to reread the sentences aloud.

This dictation procedure may seem quite long; but once it is established, five sentences can be given in ten minutes or less. The dictation provides not only drill in writing but also—and possibly even more important—training in hearing unstressed articles, final consonants, etc.—in other words, all the significant sounds of English.

For EXERCISE 7, which asks for a composition on a topic suggested by Essay 1, a student may, for instance, write a brief statement of his reaction to the essay—why he did or did not like it. Similarly, he may write on a personal experience which it recalled to him. He will doubtless use in his composition a number of words, phrases, or even entire sentences that occur in the essay. Such transference attests the value of reading in improving one's writing.

For another kind of practice, the student may be directed to write a fairly extended research paper on a related topic. That assignment can introduce him to the techniques of research and reporting, which he frequently needs in college and business. He can consult one or more reference books, learn how to take notes, organize his findings, and express them in logical fashion.

EXERCISE 8, which is a series of questions, is one of the most beneficial types of exercise, since it gives students the opportunity to hear, see, and use in different contexts most of the words and patterns of Essay 1. It further demonstrates what has been said earlier about the scope and flexibility of literate expression. The questions have all been carefully constructed so as to be natural, that is, questions that students are likely to be asked in daily life. The students should be directed to study them outside of class in order to become familiar with the written form and in order to answer them in class without looking at the book. As with Exercise 3, the questions should be spoken with normal phrasing, intonation, and speed, and the answers should be minimal: One of the greatest profits to be derived from the exercise is intensive practice in the customary manner of exchange in questioning and answering. The teacher may ask the questions or have one or two students ask them.

EXERCISE 9, which assigns an essay on one of the questions in Exercise 8, is a broadening of Exercise 7. The wealth of material in the questions offers a nearly limitless supply of topics for writing. For example, Question 1 can produce an essay on traveling, homesickness, hospitality, or first impressions; Question 2 can call forth either a reminiscence on attempting to write a play or an evaluation of the craft of playwriting. The kinds of writing may be similar to those described above in the discussion of Exercise 7.

ESSAY 2 is different from Essay 1 in that certain words and phrases are omitted from the original. Consequently, the first three exercises following Essay 2 are slightly different from those following Essay 1.

EXERCISE 10 is profitably assigned as homework. For maximum benefit, the students should copy the entire essay, not merely fill in the blanks or list the words for the blanks. Copying connected discourse increases their awareness of matters which are part of the writing system of English: spelling, capitalization, punctuation, and paragraphing. It makes visible matters such as articles, prepositions, and inflections, which many students confuse or disregard in their speaking.

In copying the essay, the students should omit the numbers in brackets so that the product will have the appearance of a customary piece of writing. If the teacher wishes, he may ask the students to underline the words which they select for the blanks.

For the reading of Essay 2, various procedures may be used. The following may be preferred, since it avoids the possibility of the students' hearing errors in the initial reading. Toward the end of a class meeting, the teacher reads the essay as it stands, pausing slightly where there is a blank and ignoring the number in the brackets before the blank. Next, he pronounces the lists of words in Exercise 10, and the students repeat them after him. To reinforce the pronunciation of the plurisyllabic words, the teacher may then wish to proceed to EXERCISE 11, pronouncing the words in the lists and having the students repeat them. Then he assigns Exercise 10 as homework. At the next meeting after the students have submitted their homework, the teacher reads the essay aloud with the correct words filled in. Exercise 11 may then be repeated. Finally, the students do EXERCISE 12: they read the essay aloud with the correct words.

EXERCISE 13 is comparable to Exercise 3 except that the questions on the essay are not listed. The teacher may compose his own, or, as a variation, he may have the students prepare questions to be asked in class. The questions may be like those in Exercise 3, which are on quite specific points and call for brief responses, or they may ask for longer answers.

The procedures discussed above can be used with all the essays and exercises in the book.

CONTENTS

MODERN ENGLISH ESSAYS

ESSAY 1 GENIUS

BY VERNON LOGGINS

In the fall of 1924 Thomas Wolfe, fresh from his courses in playwriting at Harvard, joined the eight or ten of us who were teaching freshman composition in New York University. I had never before seen a man so tall as he, so beady-eyed, and so ungraceful. I pitied him and went out of my way to help him get adjusted to his work and to make him feel at home.

His students soon let me know that he had no need of my protectiveness.

They spoke of his ability to narrate a simple event in such a manner as to have them roaring with laughter or struggling to keep back their tears, of his readiness to quote at length from any poet they could name, of his habit of writing three pages of comment on a one-page theme, and of his astonishing ease in expressing in words anything he had seen or heard or tasted or felt.

Indeed, his students made so much of his powers of observation that I decided to stage a little test and see for myself. My opportunity came one morning when the students were slowly gathering for nine-o'clock classes.

Upon arriving at the university that day, I found Wolfe alone in the large room which served all the freshman-composition teachers as an office. He made no protest when I asked him to come with me out into the hall, and he only smiled when we reached a classroom door and I bade him enter alone and look around.

He stepped in, *remained no more than thirty seconds*, and then came out. "Tell me what I see," I said as I took his place in the room, leaving him in the hall with his back to the door. Without the least hesitation and without a single error, he gave the number of seats in the room, designated those which were occupied by boys and those occupied by girls, named the colors each student was wearing, pointed out the Latin verb conjugated on the blackboard, spoke of the chalk marks which the charwoman had failed to wash from the floor, and pictured in detail the view of Washington Square from the windows.

As I rejoined Wolfe, I was speechless with amazement. He, on the contrary, was wholly calm as he said, "The worst thing about it is that I'll remember it all."

I felt no surprise whatsoever when, five years after that revealing experience, I read Wolfe's first novel, *Look Homeward, Angel*, and recognized it as perhaps the richest compendium of actually remembered sense impressions which any author had ever committed to writing.

EXERCISE 1: Pronounce the following words, emphasizing the stressed syllable by saying the vowel louder, longer, and higher in pitch than the other vowels.

A. Emphasize the first syllable of these words:

genius	poet	enter	Washington
Thomas	habit	thirty	windows
courses	writing	seconds	speechless
playwriting	pages	leaving	contrary
Harvard	comment	single	wholly
teaching	anything	error	after
freshman	tasted	number	novel
never	powers	designated	homeward
beady	little	occupied	angel
pitied	morning	colors	recognized
student	slowly	wearing	richest
simple	gathering	pointed	actually
manner	classes	Latin	author
roaring	teachers	conjugated	ever
laughter	office	blackboard	
struggling	only	charwoman	
readiness	classroom	pictures	

B. Emphasize the second syllable of these words:

before	indeed	around	experience
ungraceful	decided	remained	perhaps
adjusted	myself	without	compendium
protectiveness	o'clock	rejoined	impressions
ability	upon	amazement	committed
event	arriving	remember	
astonishing	alone	surprise	
expressing	protest	revealing	

C. Emphasize the third syllable of these words:

university	opportunity	whatsoever
observation	hesitation	

EXERCISE 2:   Read Essay 1 aloud.

EXERCISE 3:   Answer the following questions on the basis of Essay 1.

1. When did Wolfe begin teaching at New York University?
2. What college had he come from?
3. Had he been at Harvard recently?
4. What kind of courses had he been taking there?
5. How many teachers of freshman writing were there at New York University?
6. Was Wolfe a short man?
7. What kind of eyes did he have?
8. Did he have an elegant manner?
9. What first impression did Wolfe make on the author of the essay?
10. Did the author try to help him?
11. Did the author think that Wolfe knew his work?
12. Did the author think that Wolfe felt comfortable in his job?
13. Did Wolfe's students have the same feeling about him?
14. Did his students think he was a good storyteller?
15. Could he make them laugh?
16. Could Wolfe make his students want to cry?

17. Could he recite much poetry?
18. Did he seem interested in what his students wrote?
19. Was he very observant?
20. Do you think you would like to have been one of his students?
21. What did the students' comments make the author decide to do?
22. When did the author perform his experiment?
23. Where did he find Wolfe?
24. Where did the author ask Wolfe to go?
25. Did Wolfe say that he would not go?
26. What did the author ask Wolfe to do in the hall?
27. What was Wolfe's reaction to the request?
28. How long did he stay in the classroom?
29. What did the author then ask him to do?
30. Where did the author go?
31. What was Wolfe's position right then?
32. Did Wolfe have any difficulty remembering what was in the room?
33. Did he make any mistakes?
34. Did he know how many seats there were?
35. Did he know who was sitting in them?
36. Could Wolfe remember the clothes the students were wearing?
37. What was on the blackboard?
38. What was on the floor?
39. Who had not cleaned the floor?
40. What could be seen from the windows?
41. Did Wolfe remember very much about Washington Square?
42. How did the author feel at the end of the experiment?
43. Did Wolfe feel the same way?
44. Did Wolfe want to remember what he had done?
45. Was the author amazed when he read Wolfe's book?
46. When was the book published?
47. What was the title of it?
48. Did the book contain many descriptions?
49. Were they true descriptions?
50. What was the author's opinion of the book?
51. Do you think you would like to write like Wolfe?

EXERCISE 4: Give an oral summary of Essay 1.

EXERCISE 5: Write a summary of Essay 1.

EXERCISE 6: Write the parts of Essay 1 that the teacher dictates.

EXERCISE 7: Write a composition on a topic suggested by Essay 1.

EXERCISE 8: Answer the following questions, which contain words from Essay 1.

1. Are you fresh from another city?
2. Do you want to be a playwright?
3. Have you ever taken a course in freshman composition?
4. When did you first join this class?
5. Do you ever pity your teachers?
6. Do you feel grateful when someone goes out of his way to help you?
7. What sorts of things make you feel at home?
8. Do you have a feeling of protectiveness toward anyone?
9. Do you ever roar with laughter?
10. Do men usually keep back their tears?
11. Do you struggle to get awake in the morning?
12. Can you quote some poetry?
13. Do you have the habit of biting your fingernails?
14. How many words do you write for a one-page theme?
15. What do you think tastes good?
16. If I asked you to take my place, what would you do?
17. Can somebody see you if his back is to you?
18. Give me the number of students in this room.
19. Have you ever studied Latin?
20. Are there any chalk marks in this room?
21. If you feel no surprise whatsoever, how surprised are you?
22. If a book is rich, what does it contain?
23. Are you actually sure of the meaning of the word *actually?*
24. What kinds of art are concerned with sense impressions?
25. Do you have ease in expressing your thoughts in writing?
26. If a teacher bade you to be quiet, what would you do?

27. Name as many colors as you can.
28. How would you describe the view from this room?
29. Do you feel flattered when somebody makes much of a new piece of clothing that you get?
30. Does a charwoman clean your room?

EXERCISE 9: Write an essay on one of the questions in Exercise 8.

ESSAY 2 THE DETECTIVE STORY

The detective story is a popular type of fiction in which the solution of a crime is traced step by step. Edgar Allan Poe's *Murders in the Rue Morgue* is considered to be the first modern detective story, and Wilkie Collins's *The Moonstone* is the first detective novel.

In the average story the chief characters are fairly predictable. The detective, the person who unravels the mystery with [1]_____ ease in the last chapter, is customarily an eccentric [2]_____ like Sherlock Holmes, who appears in a series of adventures by the British writer Conan Doyle; or like Nero Wolfe, the corpulent, [3]_____ mastermind created by the American author Rex Stout. Nothing escapes the [4]_____ eyes of the detective, who, after a brief and apparently superficial inspection, can [5]_____ the scene of the crime in detail days or months later. Often the detective is supplied with a friend or assistant who [6]_____ the events of the story. That assistant usually possesses less acute [7]_____ of observation than the master. It is quite routine for the detective to [8]_____ a little test in which the guilty party reveals himself. In the denouement, the assistant is [9]_____ with amazement while the detective, on the contrary, is wholly calm as he [10]_____ the flaw in the criminal's plan.

EXERCISE 10: For each numbered blank in Essay 2, provide the word or phrase which best completes the meaning of the sentence. Make your selection from the numbered groups, which correspond to the numbered blanks. These lists contain words that appeared in Essay 1.

1.	2.	3.	4.
mauve	genius	ungraceful	fragrant
astonishing	comment	yonder	multitudinous
vernacular	compendium	emaciated	beady

5.	6.	7.	8.
roar	smiles	powers	stage
picture	struggles	protest	lid
bid	narrates	limelight	moisten

9.	10.
robust	commits to
speechless	delegates
tangent	points out

EXERCISE 11: Pronounce the following words, emphasizing the stressed syllable by saying the vowel louder, longer, and higher in pitch than the other vowels.

A. Emphasize the first syllable of these words:

story	fairly	nothing	comment
popular	person	after	yonder
fiction	mystery	later	fragrant
Edgar	chapter	often	beady
Allan	Sherlock	usually	picture
murders	series	master	struggles
modern	British	little	limelight
Wilkie	writer	guilty	moisten
Collins	Conan	party	speechless
moonstone	Nero	contrary	tangent
novel	corpulent	wholly	delegates
average	mastermind	criminal's	
characters	author	genius	

B. Emphasize the second syllable of these words:

detective	created	possesses	vernacular
solution	American	acute	compendium
considered	escapes	routine	ungraceful
predictable	apparently	reveals	emaciated
unravels	inspection	himself	commits
eccentric	supplied	denouement	
appears	assistant	amazement	
adventures	events	astonishing	

C. Emphasize the third syllable of these words:

superficial   customarily   observation   multitudinous

EXERCISE 12:   Read Essay 2 aloud with the blanks filled in.

EXERCISE 13:   Be prepared to answer any questions on Essay 2 that the teacher may ask.

EXERCISE 14:   Give an oral summary of Essay 2.

EXERCISE 15:   Write a summary of Essay 2.

EXERCISE 16:   Write the parts of Essay 2 that the teacher dictates.

EXERCISE 17:   Write a composition on a topic suggested by Essay 2.

EXERCISE 18:   Answer the following questions, which contain words from Essays 1 and 2.

1. Have you ever been speechless?
2. Have you ever been wholly wrong in your opinion about somebody?

3. Does a person agree with you when he says, "On the contrary"?
4. What would you recognize about a person after a revealing experience with him?
5. Can you picture a view from your childhood?
6. Would you be complimented if someone called you beady-eyed?
7. Do girls worry about being ungraceful?
8. Do men?
9. Do you like people to narrate their adventures to you?
10. How can a simple event be made to seem interesting?
11. What sort of thing astonishes you?
12. Is the power of observation a good thing to have?
13. Have you ever staged a test?
14. What did you do?
15. If you tell me something in detail, do you tell me much about it?
16. Have you gotten adjusted to attending this school?
17. What kind of person needs to be protected?
18. What ability do you think you have?
19. Are women likely to keep back their tears?
20. Are you thankful when someone shows a readiness to help you?
21. Do you have to see things for yourself before you believe them?
22. What poets can you name?
23. Do you appreciate comments on what you write?
24. When do students start to gather for this class?
25. Would you make a protest if somebody asked you to do something you did not want to do?
26. When you were a child, did you obey your mother without the least hesitation?
27. If something does not have a single error, how do you describe it?
28. Designate your left hand for me.
29. Who is occupying the seat next to you?
30. Can you conjugate a Latin verb?

EXERCISE 19: Write an essay on one of the questions in Exercise 18.

ESSAY 3 THE MARTIAN ROMANCES
BY MARK R. HILLEGAS

The last two decades of the nineteenth century were the time of the great Mars boom, a period when, as an observer noted, "public imbecility and journalistic enterprise combined to flood the papers and society with 'news from Mars.'" The boom began in 1877 with Giovanni Schiaparelli's discovery of a network of straight lines on the red planet, which he called *canali*, meaning "grooves." When the Italian word was translated into English and other languages as *canals*, the public enthusiastically responded to the implication of intelligent life, and men like Flammarion, Lowell, and Pickering developed elaborate theories about Mars and its inhabitants. The nebular hypothesis indicated to those astronomers that the outermost planets were the oldest because they were the first formed; the theory of evolution suggested that, if life began on another world, intelligent forms would eventually be produced and, given enough time, creatures superior to man would be evolved. The people of Mars had to be just such advanced beings in order to have built the great systems of canals which conserved their aging world's diminishing supply of water.

Writers turned out dozens of romances incorporating the idea that Martian civilization surpassed our own. In those stories nationalism had long before disappeared on Mars, and the planet was united as one world. The Martians were usually pictured as similar to the men on earth, though they were physically stronger and much more intelligent—only a few stories described Martians who had evolved into a nonhuman form. Forced by the increasingly adverse conditions of their older world, the Martians brought science and technology to a level of development which hovered before terrestrial men as a distant ideal. Spectacular advances were made in harnessing electricity and electromagnetic waves; radio, television, and instruments for viewing past events were already realities. Submarines, airplanes, automobiles, and conveyor-belt highways revolutionized transportation. Automation existed not only in daily life but also in manufacturing and food production. Cities became beautiful at last because of the intelligent utilization of such building materials as concrete, aluminum, and glass.

In the earliest romances enterprising adventurers from earth made the trip to Mars. In later stories the vastly superior Martians either visited our young world or invaded it, and finally in one tale the men from earth retaliated after the first Martian invasion had failed. The climax to the development of the Martian romances came with the two stories which most extensively employed the theme of invasion from space, Kurd Lasswitz's *Auf Zwei Planeten* (1897) and H. G. Wells's *The War of the Worlds* (1898). Unfortunately for the continuation of those stories into the twentieth century, new observations indicated that, whatever the explanation of the canals might be, Mars lacked sufficient oxygen and was too cold to support highly organized life forms. The idea of the Martian romances lingered on, but it never again reached the peak of popularity it had obtained in the 1890s, when the existence of the superior Martians seemed to many a very strong possibility.

EXERCISE 20: Pronounce the following words, emphasizing the stressed syllable by saying the vowel louder, longer, and higher in pitch than the other vowels.

A. Emphasize the first syllable of these words:

Martian	outermost	science	earliest
decades	oldest	level	enterprising
nineteenth	given	hovered	later
century	creatures	distant	vastly
period	people	harnessing	visited
noted	beings	radio	finally
public	systems	television	after
enterprise	aging	instruments	climax
papers	water	viewing	twentieth

network	writers	submarines	oxygen
planet	dozens	airplanes	highly
meaning	stories	automobiles	organized
English	nationalism	highways	lingered
other	usually	only	never
languages	pictured	daily	eighteen
Lowell	similar	also	nineties
Pickering	physically	cities	many
theories	stronger	beautiful	
nebular	human	building	
indicated	older	concrete	

B. Emphasize the second syllable of these words:

romances	because	described	aluminum
observer	suggested	increasingly	adventurers
combined	another	conditions	invaded
society	eventually	technology	retaliated
began	produced	development	invasion
discovery	enough	terrestrial	extensively
Italian	superior	ideal	employed
translated	evolved	spectacular	unfortunately
canals	advanced	advances	whatever
responded	conserved	events	sufficient
intelligent	diminishing	already	support
developed	supply	realities	again
elaborate	incorporating	conveyor	obtained
about	idea	existed	existence
inhabitants	surpassed	production	
hypothesis	before	became	
astronomers	united	materials	

C. Emphasize the third syllable of these words:

imbecility	disappeared	automation	popularity
journalistic	electricity	manufacturing	possibility
implication	revolutionized	observations	
evolution	transportation	explanation	

D. Emphasize the fourth syllable of these words:

enthusiastically   civilization   utilization   continuation

E. Emphasize the fifth syllable of this word:

electromagnetic

EXERCISE 21:   Read Essay 3 aloud.

EXERCISE 22:   Answer the following questions on the basis of Essay 3.

1. When were people especially interested in stories about the planet Mars?
2. Were people very intelligent in their enthusiasm?
3. Did the newspapers have anything to do with that interest?
4. What discovery aroused public interest?
5. When was that discovery made?
6. What was the nationality of the discoverer?
7. Was there any misunderstanding about that discovery?
8. Why did the English word *canal* suggest intelligent life?
9. Which planets were considered to be the oldest?
10. What was the reason for that theory?
11. Did people believe that there were live beings on the other planets?
12. Was the theory of evolution applied to that belief?
13. What was the conclusion about the level of development of those beings?
14. What did people imagine was happening to the water on Mars?
15. Why did they think that?
16. Did people think that the canal system was elaborate?
17. Were many stories written about life on Mars?
18. How did Martian civilization compare with our own?
19. Were there wars between countries on Mars?
20. Were the Martians like human beings?
21. Did all the authors think that the Martians were like men?
22. How were the physical conditions on Mars?

23. What effect did those conditions have on science and technology?
24. Did the development of science on earth equal that on Mars?
25. Did the men on earth regard the level of science on Mars as something desirable?
26. Was electricity used in homes on earth in the late nineteenth century?
27. Do we have instruments now that can reveal things as they were happening in the past?
28. Were the Martians in advance of human beings with submarines?
29. Do we have conveyor-belt highways now?
30. Do we have complete automation in use now?
31. Why were Martian cities beautiful?
32. In the earliest stories who made the trip between the planets?
33. Who made the trip in later romances?
34. Were all the trips peaceful?
35. Who were the victors in one of the latest stories?
36. What were the names of two of the most famous stories?
37. When were they written?
38. What scientific discovery made most people give up their earlier beliefs about Mars?
39. Did that discovery explain the canals?
40. Did that discovery completely stop the stories?

EXERCISE 23: Give an oral summary of Essay 3.

EXERCISE 24: Write a summary of Essay 3.

EXERCISE 25: Write the parts of Essay 3 that the teacher dictates.

EXERCISE 26: Write a composition on a topic suggested by Essay 3.

EXERCISE 27: Answer the following questions, which contain words from Essay 3.

1. Have you been in this city for a decade?
2. Which countries are famous for their systems of canals?
3. Is man a highly organized life form?
4. What does an astronomer do?
5. When do you think a telephone office is flooded with questions?
6. Do most countries try to conserve their natural resources?
7. Do most children enjoy stories about animals that can talk?
8. Where does the word *Mars* come from?
9. What are the outermost parts of a large city called?
10. Are electromagnetic waves visible?
11. What is concrete made of?
12. Are vegetables subject to evolution?
13. What wish of yours has already become a reality?
14. Is aluminum a heavy material?
15. Which period of your life are you in now?
16. How do you respond to good news?
17. Does a poor man have an adequate supply of money?
18. Does a symphony usually have more than one theme?
19. Why does a politician try to obtain popularity?
20. Are conveyor belts used for transporting?
21. What are some of the things that are found in space beyond the earth?
22. Are plants examples of intelligent life?
23. Given enough time, can almost everybody learn a second language?
24. Does an egotistical person feel vastly superior to other people?
25. Have you ever seen a planet hovering just above the horizon?
26. Is a tree a terrestrial organism?
27. Does a good workman show enterprise?
28. Can a person live without oxygen?
29. Where do you find journalistic writing?
30. Is it good for a person to have ideals even though they may be distant?

EXERCISE 28: Write an essay on one of the questions in Exercise 27.

ESSAY 4 ARCHEOLOGY

Archeology is the scientific study of the relics of man found in deposits dating from the beginnings of human life. In his science the archeologist must [1]_____ the work of historians, anthropologists, linguists, geologists, chemists, botanists, architects, engineers, and photographers. Although remains have been collected throughout historic time, notably by the Romans, the [2]_____ in archeology was initiated by the excavation of Greek sculpture after the introduction of a knowledge of ancient Greece by Greek scholars dispersed by the fall of Constantinople in 1453. Archeology has reached a [3]_____ of development in the twentieth century because [4]_____ advances have recently been made through the method of dating materials by their degree of radioactivity. Further technological development may even [5]_____ the science.

In 1832 the Danish archeologist C. J. Thomsen [6]_____ his [7]_____ that human industrial culture may be divided into stages of progress based on the [8]_____ of materials for weapons and implements. Those stages are called the Stone Age ("Paleolithic" for the early part and "Neolithic" for the later part), the Bronze Age, and the Iron Age. That sequence is accepted as true for most of the world's groups; it [9]_____ the condition of a group rather than absolute divisions of time. In different areas the succession is not synchronous, nor are the stages of equal duration. For example, some [10]_____ groups have passed directly from the Stone to the Iron Age.

EXERCISE 29:   For each numbered blank in Essay 4, provide the word or phrase which best completes the meaning of the sentence. Make your selection from the numbered groups, which correspond to the numbered blanks. These lists contain words that appeared in Essay 3.

1.	2.	3.	4.
hover	boom	jiffy	outermost
retaliate	decade	belt	nebular
incorporate	planet	peak	spectacular

5.	6.	7.	8.
note	turned out	network	nomad
evolve	invaded	theory	imbecility
revolutionize	lingered on	groove	utilization

9.	10.
conserves	enterprising
floods	adverse
indicates	languid

EXERCISE 30: Pronounce the following words, emphasizing the stressed syllable by saying the vowel louder, longer, and higher in pitch than the other vowels.

A. Emphasize the first syllable of these words:

study	knowledge	progress	hover
relics	ancient	weapons	decade
dating	scholars	implements	planet
human	twentieth	early	jiffy
science	century	later	outermost
linguists	recently	iron	nebular
chemists	methods	sequence	lingered
botanists	further	rather	network
architects	even	absolute	theory
notably	Danish	different	nomad
Romans	Thomsen	areas	indicates
sculpture	culture	synchronous	enterprising
after	stages	equal	languid

B. Emphasize the second syllable of these words:

deposits	throughout	industrial	incorporate
beginnings	historic	divided	spectacular
duration	initiated	accepted	evolve
historians	dispersed	condition	invaded
geologists	development	divisions	conserves
photographers	because	succession	adverse
although	advances	example	
remains	materials	directly	
collected	degree	retaliate	

C. Emphasize the third syllable of these words:

archeology	anthropologists	introduction	revolutionize
scientific	engineers	technological	imbecility
archeologist	excavation	neolithic	

D. Emphasize the fourth syllable of these words:

Constantinople   utilization   paleolithic

E. Emphasize the fifth syllable of this word:

radioactivity

EXERCISE 31: Read Essay 4 aloud with the blanks filled in.

EXERCISE 32: Be prepared to answer any questions on Essay 4 that the teacher may ask.

EXERCISE 33: Give an oral summary of Essay 4.

EXERCISE 34: Write a summary of Essay 4.

EXERCISE 35: Write the parts of Essay 4 that the teacher dictates.

EXERCISE 36: Write a composition on a topic suggested by Essay 4.

EXERCISE 37: Answer the following questions, which contain words from Essays 3 and 4.

1. Which century are we living in now?
2. Is wood a building material?
3. Is there a difference between a theory and a hypothesis?
4. Have we made spectacular advances in science in the last hundred years?
5. Do you think we make the maximum utilization of our natural resources?
6. Has this country had a boom recently?
7. At what hour does the temperature in the summer usually reach its peak?
8. Would you say that Columbus was enterprising?
9. Do you know how many plays Shakespeare turned out?
10. Has technology been brought to its highest possible level of development, do you think?
11. What inventions in the eighteenth century revolutionized industry?
12. What should be incorporated in the plans of a house?
13. Do you know any scientific theories?
14. Is the earth united as one world?
15. Would the owner of a newspaper be glad to be flooded with advertisements?
16. Is the top of Mount Everest too cold to support life?
17. Are you physically stronger now than you were ten years ago?
18. At most parties do some guests usually linger on after the others have gone?
19. If a person says he wants you to do something eventually, does he expect you to do it immediately?
20. Are the conditions where you are living adverse to studying?
21. Do you think that a dog is superior to a cat?
22. Have you ever been forced to do something you did not want to do?
23. Is there a strong possibility that many people will be killed in automobile accidents next year?

24. Are you flattered if a person calls something you have written "a piece of imbecility"?
25. What may evolve from an international dispute?
26. Do you suppose automation will eliminate all jobs of factory workers?
27. Has transportation advanced within the past hundred years?
28. What kind of writing has elaborate stories?
29. What instrument is used for observation of the planets?
30. How do you picture yourself twenty years from now?

EXERCISE 38: Write an essay on one of the questions in Exercise 37.

ESSAY 5   VALLEY FORGE

In the [1]_____ of a nation a few [2]_____ sites take on emotional significance for all citizens. One such spot for Americans is the small village of Valley Forge, now converted into a state park, situated on a small river in southeastern Pennsylvania some 20 miles northwest of Philadelphia. There in the American Revolution the main camp of the Continental Army was maintained from December, 1777, to June, 1778, under the command of George Washington. At the [3]_____ of the winter, [4]_____ were frightful: subsistence was wretched, barracks were not [5]_____ to accommodate the soldiers, and sickness and suffering were rife. The number of ragged and emaciated troops [6]_____ through desertion and death, and the remaining men, who totaled about eleven thousand, muttered about mutiny but were held together by their loyalty to Washington and the patriotic cause. Two distinguished foreigners, the Frenchman Lafayette and the Prussian Steuben, shared the [7]_____ misery of the soldiers. Steuben [8]_____ his energies to drilling and [9]_____ the men, [10]_____ an integrated army out of the loose-jointed band, and was with it in victory at the end of hostilities.

EXERCISE 39:   For each numbered blank in Essay 5, provide the word or phrase which best completes the meaning of the sentence. Make your selection from the numbered groups, which correspond to the numbered blanks. These lists contain words that appeared in Essays 1 to 4.

1.	2.	3.	4.
comment	historic	decade	powers
mastermind	corpulent	peak	conditions
development	synchronous	compendium	networks

5.	**6.**	**7.**	**8.**
sufficient	gathered	nebular	committed
eventual	bade	superficial	pitied
contrary	diminished	acute	quoted

9.	**10.**
roaring	evolved
organizing	struggled
revealing	dispersed

EXERCISE 40: Pronounce the following words, emphasizing the stressed syllable by saying the vowel louder, longer, and higher in pitch than the other vowels.

A. Emphasize the first syllable of these words:

valley	wretched	foreigners	corpulent
nation	barracks	Frenchman	synchronous
citizens	soldiers	Prussian	decade
village	sickness	Steuben	powers
situated	suffering	misery	networks
river	number	energies	gathered
twenty	ragged	drilling	nebular
army	totaled	jointed	pitied
under	thousand	integrated	quoted
Washington	muttered	victory	roaring
winter	mutiny	comment	organizing
frightful	loyalty	mastermind	struggle

B. Emphasize the second syllable of these words:

emotional	command	together	eventual
significance	subsistence	distinguished	diminished
American	accommodate	hostilities	acute
converted	emaciated	development	committed
southeastern	desertion	historic	revealing
northwest	remaining	compendium	evolved
maintained	about	conditions	dispersed
December	eleven	sufficient	

C. Emphasize the third syllable of these words:

Pennsylvania	revolution	patriotic	superficial
Philadelphia	continental	Lafayette	

EXERCISE 41: Read Essay 5 aloud with the blanks filled in.

EXERCISE 42: Be prepared to answer any questions on Essay 5 that the teacher may ask.

EXERCISE 43: Give an oral summary of Essay 5.

EXERCISE 44: Write a summary of Essay 5.

EXERCISE 45: Write the parts of Essay 5 that the teacher dictates.

EXERCISE 46: Write a composition on a topic suggested by Essay 5.

EXERCISE 47: Answer the following questions, which contain words from Essays 1 to 5.

1. Where does the climax come in most tales?
2. Is the number of people on earth diminishing?
3. Is it possible that people will eventually evolve into nonhuman forms?
4. Are you waiting for an opportunity to get rich?
5. Do you think that that opportunity will ever come?
6. Does the living room in your house serve as the dining room?
7. When did you first step into this room?
8. Have you ever failed to do something that you should have done?
9. Do you expect to rejoin your family soon?
10. Can you quote poetry at length?

11. Does this country have a network of highways?
12. When a man is aging, how does he feel?
13. Is steel extensively employed as a building material?
14. Does a dentist usually have a lot of instruments?
15. Do you think a man would be happy in a job if he felt he was in a groove?
16. Have you been an observer of anything interesting recently?
17. Were there many adventurers in the sixteenth century?
18. What are some of the things that you have to note when you fill out an application?
19. Do you enjoy reading a romance every now and then?
20. What is a space missile?
21. Is a man a creature?
22. If you lack money, can you go to a movie?
23. Point out the walls in this room.
24. Have you read any novels recently?
25. Can a book on grammar be called a compendium?
26. Is it hard to commit your thoughts to writing?
27. Do you ever go out of your way to help someone?
28. Is it customary for a child to retaliate after he has been struck by another child?
29. Do you think man will be able to harness the ocean to supply electricity?
30. What would give you an indication that a person was not happy?
31. Do most sons hope to surpass their fathers in education?

EXERCISE 48: Write an essay on one of the questions in Exercise 47.

ESSAY 6 HOW JOHN MILTON STUDIED LATIN

BY DONALD LEMEN CLARK

When John Milton, author of *Paradise Lost*, entered Christ's
College, Cambridge University, in 1625, he was already proficient in Latin after seven years of studying it as his second
language at St. Paul's School, London. Like all English boys
who prepared for college in grammar school, he had learned
not only to read Latin but also to speak and write it fluently
and correctly. His preparation was necessary, for all textbooks
were in Latin, and university lectures and conferences were
conducted in what was the international language of scholarship and diplomacy. His pronunciation of Latin was English,
however, and seems to have sounded strange to his friends
when he later visited Italy.

Schoolboys gained their proficiency in Latin the hard way.
They memorized rules, frequently in verses to make learning
by heart easier. When they began to read easy Latin, they
parsed the nouns and conjugated the verbs. They first made
a literal translation and then an idiomatic translation into
English. As they increased their skill, they translated their
English back into Latin without referring to the book and then
compared their versions with the original, perhaps a letter by
Cicero. The schoolmaster was always at hand to encourage and
admonish with the ferule applied to the hand or birch applied
to the seat. All schoolmasters believed Latin should be
beaten in.

After several years of study, eight hours a day, five days a
week, with review on Saturday morning, the boys began to
compose themes in imitation of the Latin authors they read,
and as they began to read Latin poetry, they began to compose
verses in Latin. Because Milton was already a poet at ten, his
verses came nearer to being poetry than those painfully put
together by the other boys. In about the fifth year at St.
Paul's School the boys commenced to study Greek, to translate
Greek into Latin, and to compose Greek prose and verses.

Still, the emphasis was on a wide reading of the best Latin authors and the composing of correct, if not inspired, Latin prose and verse.

Nevertheless, expertness in English was not neglected. The boys often first composed their themes in English, which the schoolmaster went over scrupulously before the boys made their Latin versions. And their English translations from Latin authors had to be correct and clear even if not eloquent.

During the seven years Milton spent at the university, he made constant use of his command of Latin. He wrote some excellent Latin poetry, which he published among his works in 1645. He even kept his college orations in Latin and published them with his Latin epistles in 1674.

EXERCISE 49: Pronounce the following words, emphasizing the stressed syllable by saying the vowel louder, longer, and in higher pitch than the other vowels.

A.   Emphasize the first syllable of these words:

Milton	only	conjugated	being
studied	fluently	literal	painfully
Latin	necessary	versions	other
author	lectures	letter	emphasis
paradise	conferences	Cicero	reading
entered	scholarship	master	often
college	sounded	always	scrupulously
Cambridge	later	ferule	even
after	visited	beaten	eloquent
seven	Italy	several	during
studying	memorized	study	constant
second	frequently	Saturday	excellent
language	verses	morning	published
London	learning	poetry	
English	easier	poet	
grammar	easy	nearer	

B. Emphasize the second syllable of these words:

already	increased	believed	inspired
proficient	without	review	neglected
prepared	referring	compose	before
correctly	compared	because	command
conducted	original	together	among
diplomacy	perhaps	about	orations
however	encourage	commenced	epistles
began	admonish	composing	
translation	applied	correct	

C. Emphasize the third syllable of these words:

university	preparation	international	imitation

D. Emphasize the fourth syllable of these words:

pronunciation	idiomatic	nevertheless

EXERCISE 50: Read Essay 6 aloud.

EXERCISE 51: Answer the following questions on the basis of Essay 6.

1. What is the name of one of John Milton's works?
2. Where did he go to college?
3. What century was it?
4. Did he know Latin very well?
5. Where and how long had he studied it before going to college?
6. Was Milton's training in Latin different from other boys' at that time?
7. Could he just read it?
8. Why did he need to know Latin?
9. Was his pronunciation of it the same as that of Italians?
10. Did he ever go to Italy?
11. Did schoolboys learn Latin the easy way?
12. Could they recite grammar rules from memory?
13. Why did the rules sometimes rhyme?

14. Did the students study morphology?
15. Did they translate word for word?
16. Did the students try to make their translation sound like ordinary English?
17. How did they translate their English translation back into Latin?
18. Who was one Latin author that they translated?
19. Did the teacher ever praise the boys?
20. How did he punish them?
21. What are the two meanings of *beaten in* that the author intends you to understand?
22. How many hours a day did the students study?
23. How many days a week were devoted to Latin?
24. When did the boys begin to write their own compositions in Latin?
25. Did they use Latin writers as models?
26. Did the students write their own poems in Latin?
27. When did Milton become a poet?
28. Were his youthful Latin verses very poetic?
29. When did the boys begin to study Greek?
30. Were they supposed to learn Greek very well?
31. Was the students' knowledge of Greek intended to be as deep as that of Latin?
32. Were the students expected to write good English?
33. Did they ever write compositions in English?
34. Did the schoolmaster correct their English compositions?
35. What were the requirements in their translations from Latin?
36. How long did Milton stay at Christ's College?
37. Did he use Latin outside class?
38. When did he publish his writings?
39. Was his Latin poetry very good?
40. Did he give speeches in Latin in school?
41. What did Milton later do with those speeches?

EXERCISE 52:   Give an oral summary of Essay 6.

EXERCISE 53:   Write a summary of Essay 6.

EXERCISE 54: Write the parts of Essay 6 that the teacher dictates.

EXERCISE 55: Write a composition on a topic suggested by Essay 6.

EXERCISE 56: Answer the following questions, which contain words from Essay 6.

1. Have you entered college?
2. Who is the author of *Hamlet?*
3. Are you proficient in English?
4. Can you recite any poetry that you memorized a few years ago?
5. Is a lecture similar to an oration?
6. How long do you keep your written exercises?
7. Does putting a rule into verses make it easier to remember?
8. At what age do most children learn to read?
9. Is a specialist supposed to have expertness in his subject matter?
10. What is your second language?
11. How does a pianist increase his skill?
12. Are the essays in this book written in easy English?
13. How many hours a day do you sleep?
14. Why should you go over a composition after you have written it?
15. Does your teacher ask you to parse words in this class?
16. What is the more frequent term for *schoolmaster* these days?
17. Do mothers usually want to be at hand when their children are very young?
18. Does an actor try to be eloquent?
19. Can you speak your native language fluently?
20. Who are some famous Greek authors?
21. Do you make constant use of your command of English?
22. Does it bother you if a foreigner does not speak your language correctly?
23. Which is easier for you to understand—English prose or verse?
24. What subjects are part of a student's preparation to be a physician?

25. Which side of a pair of trousers covers the seat—the front or the back?
26. Would it sound too formal to call a letter to a close friend an epistle?
27. Does a person quickly forget things that he has learned by heart?
28. After spanking a child because of a misdeed, might a mother say that the correct way has been beaten in?
29. Do most students' compositions come near to being great literature?
30. Does the hard way of learning usually turn out to be the best way?

EXERCISE 57: Write an essay on one of the questions in Exercise 56.

ESSAY 7 SEMANTICS

In one of the [1]_____ of *Romeo and Juliet*, Juliet asks the
rhetorical question "What's in a name?" and answers it with
a linguistic truism, "That which we call a rose / By any other
name would smell as sweet." In effect, she says that words are
merely conventional symbols [2]_____ objects or concepts.
Words have no direct connection with their referents; their
meaning is agreed upon by the users of a language. Therefore,
when Juliet uses the word *rose*, her audience understands that
she is [3]_____ a particular kind of flower.

Furthermore, the extension of meaning of some words is
illogical (human beings, the creators of language, are rarely
consistent). Some proper names in English can illustrate that
fact. First, the conferring of the name of Amerigo Vespucci on
the lands of the Western Hemisphere [4]_____ the dis-
coverers who preceded him. Second, the appropriation of the
title of *American* by the citizens of the United States is an
offense against logic, not to mention [5]_____. Third, the
term *Indian* cannot [6]_____ refer to the early residents of
the New World: They are quite unrelated to the [7]_____
bearers of that designation, the inhabitants of India. A little
application of [8]_____ could undoubtedly turn up in all
languages numerous other examples of the illogical use of words
which purists would [9]_____ object to and which they
would [10]_____ us not to indulge in. Nevertheless, speakers
still employ such words because there is mutual agreement on
their varied meanings.

EXERCISE 58:   For each numbered blank in Essay 7, provide the word
or phrase which best completes the meaning of the sentence. Make
your selection from the numbered groups, which correspond to the
numbered blanks. These lists contain words that appeared in Essay 6.

1.	2.	3.	4.
verses	flirted by	conducting	parses
ferules	applied to	inheriting	neglects
archetypes	warring on	referring to	inspires

5.
diplomacy
blotter
version

6.
fluently
literally
painfully

7.
proficient
original
thumbnail

8.
paradise
scholarship
birch

9.
loosely
dissimilarly
scrupulously

10.
admonish
conjugate
equate

EXERCISE 59: Pronounce the following words, emphasizing the stressed syllable by saying the vowel louder, longer, and higher in pitch than the other vowels.

A. Emphasize the first syllable of these words:

Romeo	therefore	logic	archetypes
Juliet	audience	mention	flirted
question	flower	Indian	warring
answers	furthermore	early	parses
truism	human	residents	blotter
any	beings	bearers	version
other	rarely	India	fluently
merely	proper	little	literally
symbols	English	numerous	painfully
objects	illustrate	purists	thumbnail
concepts	western	speakers	paradise
referents	hemisphere	mutual	scholarship
meaning	second	varied	loosely
users	title	verses	scrupulously
language	citizens	ferules	conjugate

B. Emphasize the second syllable of these words:

semantics	illogical	against	conducting
rhetorical	creators	refer	inheriting
linguistic	consistent	inhabitants	referring
effect	conferring	undoubtedly	neglects
conventional	Amerigo	examples	inspires

direct	Vespucci	object	diplomacy
connection	discoverers	indulge	proficient
agreed	preceded	employ	original
upon	American	because	dissimilarly
particular	united	agreement	admonish
extension	offense	applied	equate

C. Emphasize the third syllable of these words:

understands   unrelated   designation   application

D. Emphasize the fourth syllable of these words:

appropriation   nevertheless

EXERCISE 60: Read Essay 7 aloud with the blanks filled in.

EXERCISE 61: Be prepared to answer any questions on Essay 7 that the teacher may ask.

EXERCISE 62: Give an oral summary of Essay 7.

EXERCISE 63: Write a summary of Essay 7.

EXERCISE 64: Write the parts of Essay 7 that the teacher dictates.

EXERCISE 65: Write a composition on a topic suggested by Essay 7.

EXERCISE 66: Answer the following questions, which contain words from Essays 6 and 7.

1. When does a parent admonish his children?
2. Which sounds more natural—a literal translation or an idiomatic one?

3. Where do women apply rouge?
4. What kind of person composes verses as his profession?
5. Was French ever the international language of diplomacy?
6. How do you feel when you neglect a responsibility?
7. Were Germans noted for scholarship at the beginning of the twentieth century?
8. Would you go to a dentist who did his work scrupulously?
9. In what language are your current textbooks?
10. Can you read Latin poetry with ease?
11. In which century were Shakespeare's works first published?
12. Why do students learn rules about a language?
13. Do you ever compare your version of an exercise with another student's?
14. What will a child probably do if you apply a birch to his seat?
15. Would you expect to find an evil person in Paradise?
16. Does a person prepare for college in high school?
17. Was Cicero a famous painter?
18. When you were beginning to learn English, did you put sentences together painfully?
19. How many days a week do you go to school?
20. Do you like to have review before an examination?
21. Have you recently visited another country?
22. What can a teacher do to encourage a student?
23. When somebody asks you something in English, do you have to translate his words into your language and then your answer back into English?
24. Would you call Goethe's poetry inspired verse?
25. In what year are you in your study of English?
26. When does a child commence to talk?
27. In what kinds of classes do students have to compose themes?
28. Is a scholar expected to have done wide reading in his field of specialization?
29. In what language are a great number of international conferences conducted nowadays?
30. Who do you think has written excellent poetry?

EXERCISE 67: Write an essay on one of the questions in Exercise 66.

ESSAY 8 FIESTA[1]
BY WILLIAM A. OWENS

It was May, the time of fiestas.

One evening at sunset while driving in the country where I was stationed, I heard a band playing traditional folk tunes. Then, I came upon a procession marching into a village for the opening of the fiesta. On one side of the road and in perfect formation marched a band of fifteen men dressed in khaki military uniforms shinily stiff with rice starch. On the other side were thirty matrons dressed in native costumes, all especially made for the occasion and all exactly alike. The high, wide sleeves were of white hemp, heavily embroidered in red; the bodices and sarongs were light blue; the kerchiefs tied around their head peasant style were also blue. Each woman lifted her skirt on the left side just enough to show the hems of beautifully embroidered white petticoats.

The people of the village had erected a bamboo and palm arch and decorated it with crepe paper and flags. I stopped to watch. When the procession reached the arch, the band stopped too and struck up a new tune. The women formed a circle around my jeep and began to dance their folk dances for me. As they whisked around, each patted my shoulder and arm and greeted me warmly. It was all so spontaneous that I was soon returning each greeting with enthusiasm.

Then, a little old woman in a brown costume and wide rain hat came along the road. Though apparently not invited, she joined the dancing circle. Her face was old and shriveled, like a brown apple; her teeth were worn to little bits of yellow ivory set in brown, but her black eyes were lively, and she beat a light rhythm with her wooden clogs. The first time around, she caught my hand and said, "Fine, Boy." I shouted, "Fine, Mother" as loud as I could. The next time around, she said, "Boy, give me a cigarette." I handed her a pack of cigarettes. From their glances it was clear the other women regarded her as an intruder.

The music was now slow and sentimental, and the circle

[1] Revised from the version which first appeared in *Asia and the Americas*.

widened enough for two women to dance a love pantomime. The little old woman in brown stopped at one side, lit a cigarette, turned the lighted end inside her mouth as some of the women do, and smoked happily. The pantomime over, the dancers began to whirl with abandon in a fast dance.

A man who had also been watching came over and climbed in beside me. "They expect a gift for the fiesta," he said. I took some coins from my pocket and held them up. One of the women from the pantomime danced up and took them. Then, all the women danced by again, grasped my hand, and cried, "Thank you, sir." That is, all except the woman in brown. She stood and puffed her cigarette in perfect contentment.

There was a crash of drums; the band swung into "You Are My Sunshine," and they all went "trucking" into town for the fiesta.

EXERCISE 68: Pronounce the following words, emphasizing the stressed syllable by saying the vowel louder, longer, and higher in pitch than the other vowels.

A. Emphasize the first syllable of these words:

evening	matrons	patted	handed
sunset	native	shoulder	glances
driving	costumes	greeted	women
country	heavily	warmly	music
stationed	bodices	greeting	widened
playing	kerchiefs	little	pantomime
marching	peasant	dancing	lighted
village	woman	shriveled	happily
opening	lifted	apple	over
perfect	beautifully	yellow	dancers
khaki	petticoats	ivory	also
military	people	lively	watching
uniforms	decorated	rhythm	pocket
shinily	paper	wooden	sunshine
other	circle	shouted	trucking
thirty	dances	cigarette	

B. Emphasize the second syllable of these words:

fiesta	exactly	began	intruder
traditional	alike	spontaneous	inside
upon	embroidered	returning	abandon
fifteen	sarongs	enthusiasm	beside
procession	around	along	expect
formation	enough	apparently	again
especially	erected	invited	except
occasion	bamboo	regarded	contentment

C. Emphasize the third syllable of this word:

sentimental

EXERCISE 69: Read Essay 8 aloud.

EXERCISE 70: Answer the following questions on the basis of Essay 8.

1. What month was it?
2. What part of the day was it?
3. What did the author hear?
4. What kind of songs was the band playing?
5. What did he meet?
6. Where was the procession going?
7. Who were in the procession?
8. How many men were there?
9. How were they dressed?
10. How many women were there?
11. How were the women dressed?
12. Were their costumes colorful?
13. Why did the women lift their skirts?
14. What was the arch made of?
15. What was it decorated with?
16. What did the author do?
17. What did the band do when it got to the arch?
18. What did the women do?
19. What kind of automobile was the author driving?

20. Did the women touch him?
21. Did he say anything?
22. Where did the little old woman come from?
23. How was she dressed?
24. Did she dance?
25. Was she youthful looking?
26. How were her teeth?
27. Did she look sad?
28. What was she wearing on her feet?
29. What did she first say to the author?
30. Did the author respond?
31. What did she say the next time she came around in the circle?
32. What did the author give her?
33. What was the other woman's opinion of her?
34. What kind of music was played when the two women danced?
35. What sort of dance did the two women do?
36. How did the old woman smoke her cigarette?
37. Did the tempo of the music change after the pantomime?
38. Who then got into the jeep?
39. What did he say?
40. What did the author do then?
41. Who took the money?
42. What did all the women do then?
43. Did the little woman join them?
44. What did the little woman do?
45. Did the band next make a loud noise?
46. What song did it then begin to play?
47. Have you ever seen a person "trucking"—shaking his index finger and dancing?

EXERCISE 71: Give an oral summary of Essay 8.

EXERCISE 72: Write a summary of Essay 8.

EXERCISE 73: Write the parts of Essay 8 that the teacher dictates.

EXERCISE 74: Write a composition on a topic suggested by Essay 8.

EXERCISE 75: Answer the following questions, which contain words from Essay 8.

1. At what time does sunset come these days?
2. Is anyone here dressed in a uniform?
3. Have any buildings been erected around here recently?
4. Do you have many pockets in your clothes?
5. Is there usually a band in a parade?
6. Which animals supply us with ivory?
7. Do people here usually wear sarongs?
8. Are diamonds often set in rings?
9. Do coal-burning engines puff smoke?
10. Was the sky light blue this morning?
11. Are you wearing a coat over your shoulders?
12. Do you like long sleeves in the summer?
13. Have you ever decorated a Christmas tree?
14. Can you light either end of all cigarettes?
15. Is Moscow a village?
16. Is rice grown in this country, do you know?
17. Is crepe paper smooth?
18. Do you make a lot of noise when you wear wooden clogs?
19. Is a drum usually square?
20. Would you call a twelve-year-old girl a matron?
21. Are your eyes brown?
22. Do you feel like dancing when a band swings into a popular tune?
23. Do students march into this class room?
24. Why do people wear rain hats?
25. Do people truck when they dance a waltz?
26. How many hems does a dress usually have?
27. If a student goes to sleep, is he apparently not interested in the class?
28. Do all twins look exactly alike?
29. Do people form a circle when they dance some folk dances?
30. Are fresh apples usually shriveled?

EXERCISE 76: Write an essay on one of the questions in Exercise 75.

ESSAY 9 COMEDY

European comedy sprang from the boisterous rites of the
[1]_____ at the [2]_____ in honor of Dionysus in ancient
Greece. Those [3]_____ celebrations with their [4]_____
jests gave rise to dramas designed to arouse mirth. In Rome
the [5]_____ of farce, with its broad humor and absurd
exaggeration, was carried on in the plays of Plautus and
Terence. In the late Middle Ages, when the drama redevel-
oped in Europe, there were comic elements in the miracle and
morality plays, in which a [6]_____ of scenes from the Bible
was staged. The romantic comedy of the Elizabethans culmi-
nated in the plays of Shakespeare, whose comedies ranged from
farcical to tragicomic. The greatest comic and satiric playwright of France, Molière, combined the classical influence
with that of the Italian *commedia dell'arte,* which relied
heavily on the nonoral interpretation of [7]_____. In turn,
Molière's work influenced the English comedy of manners,
whose moral tone became so low that the reaction against it
resulted in the [8]_____ comedy of the eighteenth century.
Of that same time, the ballad opera, in which the action was
interspersed with songs set to [9]_____ tunes, was to be an
ancestor of the comic opera composed by Gilbert and Sullivan
and of the [10]_____ musical comedy of today.

EXERCISE 77:   For each numbered blank in Essay 9, provide the word
or phrase which best completes the meaning of the sentence. Make
your selection from the numbered groups, which correspond to the
numbered blanks. These lists contain words that appeared in Essay 8.

1.	2.	3.	4.
units	fiesta	docile	doleful
hems	khaki	jeep	spontaneous
peasants	sarong	folk	ermine

5.	6.	7.	8.
abandon	kerchief	whisk	extant
tour	sleeve	pantomime	sentimental
bodice	procession	matron	unclenched

9.	10.
shriveled	lively
bamboo	crepe
traditional	prior

EXERCISE 78:   Pronounce the following words, emphasizing the stressed syllable by saying the vowel louder, longer, and higher in pitch than the other vowels.

A. Emphasize the first syllable of these words:

comedy	elements	manners	docile
boisterous	miracle	moral	doleful
honor	Bible	century	ermine
ancient	culminated	ballad	bodice
drama	Shakespeare	opera	kerchief
humor	farcical	action	pantomime
carried	greatest	ancestor	matron
Plautus	playwright	Gilbert	shriveled
Terence	classical	Sullivan	lively
middle	influence	musical	prior
ages	heavily	units	
Europe	oral	peasants	
comic	English	khaki	

B. Emphasize the second syllable of these words:

designed	Italian	resulted	procession
arouse	*commedia*	composed	unclenched
absurd	*dell'arte*	today	bamboo
morality	relied	fiesta	traditional
romantic	became	sarong	
satiric	reaction	spontaneous	
combined	against	abandon	

C. Emphasize the third syllable of these words:

European	celebrations	tragicomic	interspersed
Dionysus	redeveloped	Molière	sentimental

D. Emphasize the fourth syllable of these words:

exaggeration   Elizabethans   interpretation

EXERCISE 79: Read Essay 9 aloud with the blanks filled in.

EXERCISE 80: Be prepared to answer any questions on Essay 9 that the teacher may ask.

EXERCISE 81: Give an oral summary of Essay 9.

EXERCISE 82: Write a summary of Essay 9.

EXERCISE 83: Write the parts of Essay 9 that the teacher dictates.

EXERCISE 84: Write a composition on a topic suggested by Essay 9.

EXERCISE 85: Answer the following questions, which contain words from Essays 8 and 9.

1. Does a sad person have a lively expression?
2. Is a person silent when he performs a pantomime?
3. Are folk tunes the kind of songs you usually hear over the radio?
4. When somebody steps on your toes, do you give a spontaneous cry?
5. Do people usually walk fast in a procession?
6. Is a fiesta the same as a feast?

7. Are peasant-style dresses usually worn at a formal occasion?
8. Does a dignified person do many things with abandon?
9. Do you like slow and sentimental music when you are relaxing?
10. Can you play a musical instrument?
11. When is this class over?
12. What are the colors of your national flag?
13. Is the month of May warm here?
14. Do you think that women's skirts should be longer?
15. Will a person get dizzy if he whirls around many times?
16. Do you watch television very much?
17. Have you ever kept a favorite piece of clothing until it was worn to rags?
18. Do you regard all the people you know as your close friends?
19. Is a bodice a kind of coat?
20. Are chorus girls supposed to dance in perfect formation?
21. When you see an unfriendly dog, do you stop and pat him?
22. Does a military band usually play love songs?
23. On which part of the body is a kerchief worn?
24. Do brides usually have dresses especially made for their weddings?
25. Were you here at the opening of this school year?
26. Do you see many jeeps these days?
27. What kinds of persons are stationed in a foreign country?
28. Have you ever seen a chair made of bamboo?
29. Do people whisk around when they dance a polka?
30. Did your mother tell you any traditional stories when you were young?

EXERCISE 86: Write an essay on one of the questions in Exercise 85.

ESSAY 10   A CITIZEN

A citizen is a member of a state or nation who owes allegiance to a government and is entitled to its protection. A person may be a citizen by birth (a [1]_____) or may become one through naturalization (a naturalized citizen). Citizens are [2]_____ differentiated from nonnationals who reside in a state—that is, aliens. In former times, however, citizens were [3]_____ as different from subjects with a servile status—for example, slaves and serfs. In [4]_____ Greece, property owners in the city-states were citizens. As such they might vote and were liable for taxes and [5]_____ service. In the Roman Empire, citizenship, at first limited to [6]_____ of the city of Rome, was extended by A.D. 212 to all free [7]_____ of the empire. Under feudalism the [8]_____ of national citizenship ceased to exist in Europe. In time, burgesses purchased the immunity of their cities from feudal dues and thereby achieved a privileged position and a power in local government; those community rights were akin to citizenship and [9]_____ in later legislation respecting citizenship. Now each country determines the structure of its citizenship laws. In some countries citizenship [10]_____ with the *jus sanguinis* ("law of blood"), whereby a child if legitimate takes its citizenship from its father and if illegitimate from its mother. In other countries the *jus soli* ("law of soil") governs, and citizenship is determined by the place of birth.

EXERCISE 87:   For each numbered blank in Essay 10, provide the word or phrase which best completes the meaning of the sentence. Make your selection from the numbered groups, which correspond to the numbered blanks. These lists contain words that appeared in Essays 6 to 9.

1.	2.	3.	4.
hamlet	hastily	overcome	ancient
design	conventionally	regarded	conjugated
native	uncooperatively	shriveled	mutual

5.	6.	7.	8.
relied	residents	notions	concept
khaki	frictions	inhabitants	indigent
military	capacities	terms	ballad

9.	10.
preceded	agrees
culminated	indulges
admonished	neglects

EXERCISE 88: Pronounce the following words, emphasizing the stressed syllable by saying the vowel louder, longer, and higher in pitch than the other vowels.

A. Emphasize the first syllable of these words:

citizen	liable	power	ancient
member	taxes	local	conjugated
nation	service	government	mutual
government	Roman	later	khaki
person	empire	country	military
naturalized	citizenship	structure	residents
aliens	limited	father	frictions
former	under	mother	notions
different	feudalism	other	concept
subjects	national	*soli*	indigent
servile	Europe	governs	ballad
status	burgesses	hamlet	culminated
property	purchased	native	
owners	feudal	hastily	
city	privileged	shriveled	

B. Emphasize the second syllable of these words:

allegiance	extended	respecting	relied
entitled	exist	determine	capacities
protection	immunity	*sanguinis*	inhabitants
become	thereby	whereby	preceded

nonnationals	achieved	legitimate	admonished
reside	position	design	agrees
however	community	conventionally	indulges
example	akin	regarded	neglects

C. Emphasize the third syllable of these words:

| differentiated | illegitimate | overcome |
| legislation | uncooperatively | |

D. Emphasize the fifth syllable of this word:

naturalization

EXERCISE 89: Read Essay 10 aloud with the blanks filled in.

EXERCISE 90: Be prepared to answer any question on Essay 10 that the teacher may ask.

EXERCISE 91: Give an oral summary of Essay 10.

EXERCISE 92: Write a summary of Essay 10.

EXERCISE 93: Write the parts of Essay 10 that the teacher dictates.

EXERCISE 94: Write a composition on a topic suggested by Essay 10.

EXERCISE 95: Answer the following questions, which contain words from Essays 6 to 10.

1. Have you made a tour of this country?
2. After a good dinner do you have a feeling of perfect contentment?

3. Can you beat a rhythm with your fingers?
4. Do cooks frequently tie aprons around their waists?
5. As you increase your proficiency in English, do you find that you do not need to refer to a dictionary as often as you used to?
6. Are most English verbs easy to conjugate?
7. Do men in this city usually wear heavily embroidered shirts?
8. Is a person an intruder when he goes to a party to which he has not been invited?
9. Do you usually feel stiff after you have been sitting for a long time?
10. Is a grammar school the same in the United States as in England, do you know?
11. Is anyone in this room dressed in khaki?
12. Should many streets in this city be widened?
13. Have you ever seen the Arch of Triumph in Paris?
14. Why do some men have starch in their collars?
15. Would an American be flattered if you told him his pronunciation of French was English?
16. Is a palm leaf broad or narrow?
17. Do you sometimes jump when you hear a loud crash of thunder?
18. Do women usually wear many petticoats nowadays?
19. Do children often shout when they get excited playing a game?
20. How long did it take you not only to read English but also to speak and write it?
21. When somebody helps you, do you want to return the favor?
22. Are there many signs along the streets in this city?
23. Do nonsmokers usually carry packages of cigarettes?
24. Does a band strike up a tune when it begins playing or when it ends playing?
25. Does it sometimes sound strange to make a literal translation from one language into another?
26. Are you glad when you come upon some money you had forgotten you had?
27. Did native speakers' pronunciation of English sound strange to you when you first heard it?
28. Can you sometimes tell from a teacher's glance that he is not pleased with something you have done?

29. Why does a person have to work hard to gain proficiency in a second language?
30. Do most children learn to speak through imitation of their parents and other relatives?

EXERCISE 96: Write an essay on one of the questions in Exercise 95.

ESSAY 11 SIMPLICITY IN SHAKESPEARE

BY ERNEST BRENNECKE

Shakespeare has held the stage for about four hundred years. He is today the most often produced of playwrights, the most intensively studied poet in the world. Many millions of words have been poured out expounding his subtleties and complexities. However, subtlety and complexity cannot explain an artist's firm hold on the minds and emotions of countless ordinary persons.

There is one recurrent virtue in Shakespeare's work which has been largely overlooked, even drowned under oceans of involved speculation. That is the virtue of sheer simplicity. Let me illustrate with a few passages.

A young man is searching for his twin brother from whom he has been separated since infancy. How does he put his situation? "I to the world am like a drop of water that in the ocean seeks another drop." (*Comedy of Errors*, I, ii, 35)

A girl expresses her lifelong attachment to her friend: "So we grew together, like . . . a double cherry, seeming parted, . . . two lovely berries molded on one stem." (*Midsummer Night's Dream*, III, ii, 208)

Hundreds of such charming examples of the appeal to the simple experiences of common life could be cited. But what about the more serious and grim situations?

A friend of Mark Antony, revolted by his general's infatuation with Cleopatra, exclaims, "His captain's heart, which to the scuffles of great fights hath burst the buckles of his breast, . . . is become the bellows and the fan to cool a gipsy's lust!" (*Antony and Cleopatra*, I, i, 6)

When Hamlet is asked where is the body of Polonius, whom he has slain, he answers, "At supper. Not where he eats, but where he is eaten: . . . worms are e'en at him." (*Hamlet*, IV, iii, 20)

Finally, when a monstrous villain stamps out the eye of his helpless victim, he shouts, "Out, vile jelly!" (*Lear*, IV, i, 83)

Of course, Shakespeare is by no means always so plain. In his work there are many profundities which will perplex us for a long time to come. Nevertheless, in many of his most telling moments, while he runs through the gamut of human joy and suffering, from the airiest lyric romance to the ultimate in horror, his power exhibits itself with a startling clarity—a simplicity which supplies us with one of the many proper explanations of his enduring appeal.

EXERCISE 97: Pronounce the following words, emphasizing the stressed syllable by saying the vowel louder, longer, and higher in pitch than the other vowels.

A. Emphasize the first syllable of these words:

Shakespeare	illustrate	simple	villain
hundred	passages	common	helpless
often	searching	cited	victim
playwrights	brother	serious	jelly
studied	separated	Antony	always
poet	infancy	general's	telling
many	water	captain's	moments
millions	comedy	scuffles	gamut
subtlety	errors	buckles	human
artist's	double	bellows	suffering
countless	cherry	gipsy's	airiest
ordinary	seeming	Hamlet	lyric
persons	parted	body	ultimate
virtue	lovely	answers	horror
largely	berries	supper	power
even	molded	eaten	startling
under	midsummer	finally	clarity
ocean	charming	monstrous	proper

B. Emphasize the second syllable of these words:

simplicity	explain	examples	perplex
about	emotions	appeal	exhibits
today	recurrent	experiences	itself

produced	involved	revolted	supplies
intensively	another	exclaims	enduring
expounding	expresses	become	
complexity	attachment	Polonius	
however	together	profundities	

C. Emphasize the third syllable of these words:

| overlooked | situation | explanations |
| speculation | Cleopatra | |

D. Emphasize the fourth syllable of these words:

| infatuation | nevertheless |

EXERCISE 98: Read Essay 11 aloud.

EXERCISE 99: Answer the following questions on the basis of Essay 11.

1. How long has Shakespeare been popular?
2. Are his plays often performed?
3. Is he considered to be a poet?
4. Has much been written to explain what is obscure and complicated in his plays?
5. Do his subtleties and complexities explain his popularity?
6. What is one excellent quality of Shakespeare's that has frequently been disregarded by critics?
7. In the *Comedy of Errors,* whom is the young man looking for?
8. Has he seen that person recently?
9. To what does he compare himself and his brother?
10. In *A Midsummer Night's Dream,* what is the young woman talking about?
11. To what does she compare herself and her friend?
12. Does Shakespeare have many references to ordinary things?
13. In the passage from *Antony and Cleopatra,* does his friend approve of Antony's love for Cleopatra?
14. Does that friend think that Antony has been brave in battles?

15. To whom is Antony now giving his attention?
16. Does his friend have a high opinion of Cleopatra?
17. In the scene from *Hamlet,* what has Hamlet done recently?
18. How does he say that Polonius is dead?
19. In the passage from *Lear,* what does the horribly bad man do?
20. What does he call his victim's eye?
21. Does Shakespeare always use simple language?
22. Are there any unclear passages in his plays?
23. Is he easily understood in many of his most effective incidents?
24. Does he portray many human emotions?
25. Is his surprising clearness one of the reasons for his lasting popularity?

EXERCISE 100:　Give an oral summary of Essay 11.

EXERCISE 101:　Write a summary of Essay 11.

EXERCISE 102:　Write the parts of Essay 11 that the teacher dictates.

EXERCISE 103:　Write a composition on a topic suggested by Essay 11.

EXERCISE 104:　Answer the following questions, which contain words from Essay 11.

1. What new invention is holding the world's stage right now?
2. Is a beautiful girl lovely to look at?
3. How many meals have you eaten today?
4. Is a playwright happy when his plays are produced?
5. What kinds of berries do you like?
6. Does a policeman often encounter grim situations?
7. Do many religious statements contain profundities?
8. In a large crowd do you sometimes feel like a drop of water?
9. Is a monstrous villain a likable sort of fellow?
10. Who are some world-famous politicians?

11. Are plain directions easy to follow?
12. Do men here carry fans very often?
13. When does spring begin to exhibit itself here?
14. What are college students supposed to be seeking?
15. What means are used to cool a house?
16. Does a diplomat usually express his feeling with startling clarity?
17. What can illustrate a person's character?
18. Does a calm person exclaim very often?
19. Is a fine actress supposed to be able to run through the gamut of emotions?
20. Do you remember any passages from the last story you have read?
21. Is a captain superior in rank to a private?
22. Does a person ordinarily express joy by crying?
23. Are you pleased when you overlook something you need?
24. Does a beggar make an appeal to your sympathy?
25. Does the English language contain any complexities for you?
26. Are there many cherry trees in Japan?
27. Do you suppose that a postman sometimes feels that he is surrounded by oceans of letters?
28. Is rain a common occurrence in this part of the country?
29. Is a great singer sometimes called an artist?
30. What article of men's clothing has a buckle?
31. Which does a history book usually appeal to—your mind or your emotions?
32. Is a horror story about a pleasant incident?
33. Have you ever used a bellows to make a fire burn more intensely?
34. Are there some heroes who are considered to be shining examples for young people?
35. Does a general have a low position in an army?
36. Is the moon a recurrent object in the sky?
37. Is a six-month-old dog as helpless as a six-month-old child?
38. Is the ability to concentrate a virtue for a student?
39. Do we call a person from Egypt a gipsy these days?
40. Can you always understand a subtlety right away?

EXERCISE 105: Write an essay on one of the questions in Exercise 104.

ESSAY 12 UTOPIA

Though the concept of an earthly paradise was not given the appellation of Utopia until the sixteenth century by Sir Thomas More, the idea has doubtless had a firm [1]_____ on men's imagination since the beginning of cogitation. [2]_____ social, religious, political, and economic philosophers and visionaries—including Plato, St. Augustine, Bacon, Rabelais, and Rousseau, have been [3]_____ by the inhumanity of man and the inequalities in society and have drawn up their schemes for an ideal state where no man is [4]_____ and from which [5]_____ has been banished. Some such thinkers have [6]_____ their theories with simplicity, and others have indulged in [7]_____ speculation.

Utopian works have had an immense force in the history of thought, but their influence has been [8]_____ inspirational rather than practical, since most of the draftsmen of a perfect order have not [9]_____ the details of the means whereby human beings could be prevailed upon to change their habits and patterns of thought and so arrive at the blessed land of no more sin or anguish. As a matter of fact, the very word *utopian* has fallen into disrepute in some quarters and is often employed contemptuously to denote [10]_____ impracticality. The notion of an Eden created by man has been treated comically or satirically by a throng of writers, among them Aristophanes, Jonathan Swift, Aldous Huxley, and George Orwell.

EXERCISE 106: For each numbered blank in Essay 12, provide the word or phrase which best completes the meaning of the sentence. Make your selection from the numbered groups, which correspond to the numbered blanks. These lists contain words that appeared in Essay 11.

1.	2.	3.	4.
hold	twin	poured	vile
subtlety	countless	cited	airy
stem	recurrent	revolted	ultimate

5.	6.	7.	8.
gamut	perplexed	parted	largely
buckle	smoldered	slain	stonily
suffering	expounded	involved	plushly

9.	10.
scuffled	sheer
rent	pebbly
supplied	sagacious

EXERCISE 107: Pronounce the following words, emphasizing the stressed syllable by saying the vowel louder, longer, and higher in pitch than the other vowels.

A. Emphasize the first syllable of these words:

concept	others	very	countless
earthly	history	fallen	cited
paradise	influence	into	airy
given	rather	quarters	ultimate
century	practical	often	gamut
Thomas	draftsmen	notion	buckle
doubtless	perfect	Eden	suffering
social	order	treated	smoldered
visionaries	human	comically	parted
Plato	beings	writers	largely
Augustine	habits	Jonathan	stonily
Bacon	patterns	Aldous	scuffled
banished	blessed	Huxley	plushy
thinkers	anguish	Orwell	pebbly
theories	matter	subtlety	

B. Emphasize the second syllable of these words:

utopia	Rousseau	prevailed	among
until	society	upon	recurrent
idea	ideal	arrive	revolted
beginning	simplicity	employed	perplexed
religious	indulged	contemptuously	expounded
political	utopian	denote	involved
philosophers	immense	created	supplied
including	whereby	satirically	sagacious

C. Emphasize the third syllable of these words:

appellation	inhumanity	inspirational
cogitation	inequalities	disrepute
economic	speculation	Aristophanes

D. Emphasize the fourth syllable of these words:

imagination	impracticality

EXERCISE 108: Read Essay 12 aloud with the blanks filled in.

EXERCISE 109: Be prepared to answer any questions on Essay 12 that the teacher may ask.

EXERCISE 110: Give an oral summary of Essay 12.

EXERCISE 111: Write a summary of Essay 12.

EXERCISE 112: Write the parts of Essay 12 that the teacher dictates.

EXERCISE 113: Write a composition on a topic suggested by Essay 12.

EXERCISE 114: Answer the following questions, which contain words from Essays 11 and 12.

1. Have you been in this country since infancy?
2. Does a theoretician spend much time in speculation?
3. Are there countless fish in the ocean?
4. Would you feel flattered if somebody said you had done something through sheer stupidity?
5. When a person is seasick, is he revolted by the sight of blood?
6. Can an author express his ideas clearly by means of simplicity?
7. Does a teacher of science expound theories?
8. Does a person compliment you when he calls you a vile name?
9. Is a comedy usually about suffering?
10. Is your life largely made up of simple experiences?
11. Does a dictator wish to keep a firm hold on his subjects?
12. Does a teacher of literature frequently cite examples from authors?
13. Which would be the more likely subject of a lyric romance— a pleasant story about young people or a tale about the murder of a king?
14. What do you call a person who molds figures?
15. Do apples have stems?
16. How many millions of persons are there in the world today, do you guess?
17. Do you enjoy a play that has telling scenes?
18. Do you like a charming picture?
19. What elements is the world's atmosphere largely made of?
20. Is lust a noble emotion?
21. Whom should you ask to help you when you are searching for a missing person?
22. Can a person be tried for murder if the body of his victim cannot be found?
23. Would you like to be a twin?
24. Is jelly a hard substance?
25. Do many men part their hair on the left side?
26. Do some theories in physics seem very involved to you?
27. Does the effectiveness of a story depend on how the author puts the situation?
28. Does a mystery perplex you?

29. Have you ever had to stamp out a cigarette with your foot?
30. Is an infatuation based on reason?
31. When you hurt somebody, are you called the victim?
32. Do you find examples of usage in a grammar book?
33. Do you feel an attachment to your closest friend?
34. Has anyone ever talked to you so much that you felt drowned in words?
35. Does a gay person have an airy attitude?
36. Do you call your evening meal your dinner or your supper?
37. Do people use worms when they go fishing, do you know?
38. Do you hope you will live for a long time to come?
39. Can a person express his feelings just by a look on his face?
40. Do you like people who shout into your ear?

EXERCISE 115: Write an essay on one of the questions in Exercise 114.

ESSAY 13 SCALLOPS

BY HAROLD E. PAGLIARO

Marine biologists distinguish between many varieties of scallops, all of which are mollusks belonging to one family. People who are more interested in the culinary than in the scientific classification of those bivalves, however, need know only the difference between sea scallops and bay scallops. Although in both varieties the single muscle, which holds together the radially ribbed shells, is traditionally the edible part of the animal (sea gulls have other views), the sea scallop yields a rather tough, stringy cylinder of meat, perhaps an inch in height and an inch and a half in diameter, whereas the bay scallop of the same region, typically less than a third the size of its cousin, is usually tender and sweet.

Some time in late September or early October thousands upon thousands of the bay scallops, helped by currents—and in the shallows, by winds as well—move lazily but inexorably from outside waters to the quiet bays and creeks of northern and eastern Long Island. At that time of year the casual beach stroller can see them lapping at the shore as they clap their flesh-lined shells open and shut, like the lips of so many forlorn mouths. It takes very little effort then to wade knee-deep in the usually calm waters of Indian summer and gather up enough for dinner. All one has to do is move along, popping scallops into a bucket or bushel basket as he goes. The amiable mollusks protest with only a mild, gurgling growl as they discharge air and water through their gnashing gums. Since it takes no more than 3 dozen to satisfy even a full-grown human male, the job is soon done.

Preparing bay scallops for cooking is a very minor art. After the operator has lightly rinsed the bivalve if it was gathered from a muddy bottom, he gently pries the undulated edges of the loosely joined shells apart with a knife (the job takes little strength or skill) and uses his free thumb to keep them separated. Then, he inserts the knife so that the cutting edge, which should be flexible, follows the inner surface of the upper shell and frees one end of the edible muscle. Next, he passes his blade around the edge of the lower shell, between the flesh surrounding the edible "eye," as professional scallopers call the muscle, and the inside of the shell, being careful not to touch the eye: Poor surgery makes a chore out of the otherwise easy and satisfying job of separating the entrails from the muscle. As the deft surgeon finishes his pass around the fringes of the lower shell, he hooks his knife under the loop of flesh he has loosened and tugs upward, leaving a quivering and succulent white morsel lightly fastened to the mother-of-pearl background.

After they are separated from their shells, scallops may be broiled in butter or dipped in flour and seasoned batter and fried. They are delicious both ways, and so the gourmet will not concern himself with the choice open to him: He will already have made the only significant choice in preferring bay to sea scallops.

EXERCISE 116: Pronounce the following words, emphasizing the stressed syllable by saying the vowel louder, longer, and higher in pitch than the other vowels.

A. Emphasize the first syllable of these words:

scallop	cousin	summer	lightly
many	usually	gather	muddy
mollusks	tender	dinner	bottom
family	early	popping	gently
people	thousands	bucket	undulated
interested	currents	bushel	edges
culinary	shallows	basket	loosely
bivalve	lazily	amiable	little
difference	outside	only	uses
single	water	gurgling	separated
muscle	quiet	gnashing	cutting
radially	northern	dozen	flexible
edible	eastern	satisfy	follows

animal	island	even	inner
other	casual	human	surface
rather	stroller	cooking	upper
stringy	lapping	very	passes
cylinder	open	minor	lower
region	effort	after	scallopers
typically	Indian	operator	inside
being	entrails	leaving	background
careful	surgeon	quivering	separated
surgery	finishes	succulent	butter
otherwise	fringes	morsel	seasoned
easy	under	lightly	batter
satisfying	loosened	fastened	gourmet
separating	upward	mother	

B. Emphasize the second syllable of these words:

marine	traditionally	enough	professional
biologists	perhaps	along	delicious
distinguish	diameter	protest	concern
between	whereas	discharge	himself
varieties	September	preparing	already
belonging	October	apart	significant
however	upon	inserts	preferring
although	inexorably	around	
together	forlorn	surrounding	

C. Emphasize the third syllable of this word:

scientific

D. Emphasize the fourth syllable of this word:

classification

EXERCISE 117: Read Essay 13 aloud.

EXERCISE 118: Answer the following questions on the basis of Essay 13.

1. According to scientific classification, are there many kinds of scallops?
2. What is the name of the large group of animals that scallops belong to?
3. How many kinds of scallops does a person interested in cooking know?
4. Why is a scallop called a bivalve?
5. What is the function of the muscle?
6. What design do the shells have?
7. Which part of the scallop does a person eat?
8. What are the differences between the bay scallop and the sea scallop?
9. When do the bay scallops appear near land?
10. Are there many of them then?
11. What helps the bay scallops move?
12. Do they move fast?
13. Do they move steadily?
14. Where do they appear on Long Island?
15. Are they easily visible?
16. What action do the scallops perform?
17. What do they remind the author of?
18. Is it difficult to collect them?
19. Do the scallops struggle when they are taken?
20. How many constitute a full meal?
21. Is it easy to prepare scallops for cooking?
22. What kind of scallop is washed?
23. What instrument is used to force the shells open?
24. How is a thumb used?
25. Should a knife with a stiff blade be used?
26. How is the part that is eaten detached from the shell?
27. What is the trade term for the muscle?
28. Can an inexpert person have trouble removing the eye?
29. What color is the eye?
30. In what ways may scallops be cooked?

EXERCISE 119: Give an oral summary of Essay 13.

EXERCISE 120: Write a summary of Essay 13.

EXERCISE 121: Write the parts of Essay 13 that the teacher dictates.

EXERCISE 122: Write a composition on a topic suggested by Essay 13.

EXERCISE 123: Answer the following questions, which contain words from Essay 13.

1. Do you have a single thumb on your hand?
2. How do you move along when you are tired?
3. Is your arm loosely joined to your shoulder?
4. Do you customarily eat just one morsel of meat at dinner?
5. Which is more of a cylinder—a cigarette or a banana?
6. Why can a surgeon be called an operator?
7. What holds your lips together?
8. Do you have no more than two eyes?
9. Does a bald man have to think about passing a comb through his hair?
10. Do you prefer ice cream to pie as a dessert?
11. Do you like to go wading in the shallows along a beach?
12. At what age is a person full-grown?
13. Is your flesh above or beneath your skin?
14. What are some of the animals that belong to the mollusk group?
15. When you wake in the morning, do you like to move lazily in your bed before you get up?
16. Is a human male as strong as an elephant?
17. Does it take much skill to be a professional ice skater?
18. Are most men's belts flexible?
19. What are the edges of your front teeth used for?
20. Is a thoughtful person careful not to offend other people?
21. What is the scientific classification of human beings?
22. Can you swim in water that is knee-deep?
23. Does the smell of cooking sometimes arouse your appetite?
24. Who performs surgery in a hospital?

25. Is a mussel a bivalve?
26. Do you act casual when somebody tells you a piece of bad news?
27. Do you ever gnash your teeth when you are angry?
28. Do imaginative children often make a game out of a chore?
29. When do you gather up your books and leave this room?
30. Do you know when the period of Indian summer is?
31. Are the cuffs of men's shirts usually undulated?
32. Which would you more likely describe as quivering—a portion of jelly or a piece of meat?
33. When you eat stringy meat, do particles of it sometimes stick between your teeth?
34. Would you say that wrapping presents attractively is a very minor art?
35. Does a high school graduate intending to go to college have any choice open to him?
36. When you look at the bathers on a large beach, do there seem to be thousands upon thousands?
37. How would you feel if you saw a man running toward you with a knife?
38. Are your ears lightly fastened to your head?
39. Have you ever had to carry buckets of water because the faucets in your house were not working?
40. Does a good pianist have to be deft?

EXERCISE 124: Write an essay on one of the questions in Exercise 123.

ESSAY 14 MONEY

Today almost all economic activity is [1]_____ with the making and spending of money. An astonishing [2]_____ of objects have served as money—for example, stones, shells, ivory, wampum beads, tobacco, furs, dried fish, and cigarettes. It is [3]_____ that both in Latin and in Anglo-Saxon the word for cattle also denoted money. Precious metals have [4]_____ had wide monetary use because of their convenience of handling, durability, divisibility, and the high intrinsic value commonly attached to them. Once an article is accepted as a medium of exchange, however, the tendency is to cease [5]_____ between the article's face value and its commodity value; the only criterion is that the degree of exchangeability will [6]_____ sellers' desire for reward for goods and services.

Research has [7]_____ the indication that state coinage originated in Lydia during the seventeenth century B.C., and the practice slowly but [8]_____ spread throughout the world. Paper currency first appeared about three hundred years ago; it was [9]_____ backed by some standard commodity into which it could be freely converted on demand, but even in the early days issuance of inconvertible paper money was not infrequent. Since 1934, gold has served in the United States as the standard of value, but it may no longer be used as a domestic medium of exchange. The country's gold stock has been [10]_____ by the Federal government, and it is now illegal for private persons or firms to possess gold except for specified export or industrial purposes.

EXERCISE 125: For each numbered blank in Essay 14, provide the word or phrase which best completes the meaning of the sentence. Make your selection from the numbered groups, which correspond to the numbered blanks. These lists contain words that appeared in Essay 13.

1.	2.	3.	4.
strolled	variety	marine	stringily
concerned	bivalve	forlorn	culinarily
tripled	bay	significant	traditionally

5.	6.	7.	8.
lapping	satisfy	ribbed	edibly
gurgling	pop	yielded	inexorably
distinguishing	gnash	clapped	succulently

9.	10.
typically	waded around
radially	gathered up
edgily	rinsed off

EXERCISE 126: Pronounce the following words, emphasizing the stressed syllable by saying the vowel louder, longer, and higher in pitch than the other vowels.

A. Emphasize the first syllable of these words:

money	value	hundred	tripled
making	commonly	standard	bivalve
spending	article	into	stringily
objects	medium	freely	lapping
ivory	tendency	even	gurgling
wampum	only	early	satisfy
cigarettes	sellers	issuance	yielded
Latin	services	longer	edibly
Anglo-	coinage	country's	succulently
Saxon	Lydia	federal	typically
cattle	during	government	radially
also	century	private	edgily
precious	practice	persons	waded
metals	slowly	specified	gathered
monetary	paper	export	
handling	currency	purposes	

B.   Emphasize the second syllable of these words:

today	exchange	about	concerned
activity	however	ago	variety
astonishing	between	converted	marine
example	commodity	demand	forlorn
tobacco	criterion	infrequent	significant
denoted	degree	united	traditionally
because	desire	domestic	distinguishing
convenience	reward	illegal	inexorably
intrinsic	originated	possess	
attached	throughout	except	
accepted	appeared	industrial	

C.   Emphasize the third syllable of these words:

economic	indication	inconvertible
durability	culinarily	

D.   Emphasize the fourth syllable of these words:

divisibility	exchangeability

EXERCISE 127:   Read Essay 14 aloud with the blanks filled in.

EXERCISE 128:   Be prepared to answer any questions on Essay 14 that the teacher may ask.

EXERCISE 129:   Give an oral summary of Essay 14.

EXERCISE 130:   Write a summary of Essay 14.

EXERCISE 131:   Write the parts of Essay 14 that the teacher dictates.

EXERCISE 132:   Write a composition on a topic suggested by Essay 14.

Answer the following questions, which contain words from Essays 13 and 14.

1. What plant yields linen?
2. How much food does it take to satisfy your hunger in the morning?
3. What is the most significant choice that a college student has to make in regard to his education?
4. Are there many varieties of snakes?
5. Do you have any culinary skill?
6. Is the peel traditionally the edible part of an orange?
7. Are you inexorably opposed to learning new facts?
8. Where do the organisms in which a marine biologist is interested live?
9. How many sets of gums do you have?
10. Do you still have difficulty distinguishing between certain English sounds?
11. What is your height?
12. Why should you rinse fresh vegetables?
13. Is a scallop related to an oyster?
14. Would you be more likely to get your lips chapped in summer than in winter?
15. Does it take much skill to be an aviator?
16. How many animals do you know that have shells?
17. Is it difficult to get along with amiable people?
18. Which is more expensive—butter or oleomargarine?
19. When you were a child, did you protest when your hair was cut?
20. How many loops do you make when you tie a shoelace?
21. Do bears and monkeys generally live in the same region?
22. Do you like to be awakened gently in the morning?
23. Do you know how to make batter for pancakes?
24. Is a male bird usually more colorful than a female?
25. Have you ever tried to pry a watch case apart?
26. Should a sick person eat highly seasoned food?
27. Have you ever seen a whale discharge air when it came to the surface?
28. If a person gets angry, can he spoil an otherwise pleasant party?

29. Is it all right to clap a door shut in a hospital?
30. What do your muscles let you do with your arm?
31. Do you have to free a banana from its skin before you eat it?
32. Does it take much strength to lift a bicycle?
33. Is your thumb longer than an inch?
34. Have you heard the song about the surrey with the fringe on top?
35. Does a happy person usually feel forlorn?
36. Where do gulls live?
37. If you put your finger in the palm of a baby's hand, will he hook his fingers around yours?
38. How much time does preparing for this class take you?
39. Are the waters in a whirlpool calm?
40. Do you enjoy it when a dentist tugs at one of your teeth that he is trying to extract?

EXERCISE 134: Write an essay on one of the questions in Exercise 133.

ESSAY 15 ASTRONOMY

For ages the heavenly bodies have [1]_____ both to man's imagination and to his desire for knowledge. Naturally, today's mechanical devices for flights into space have increased the interest in astronomy greatly. The ancients depicted the universe in a [2]_____ of ways but essentially conceived it as a valley surrounded by insurmountable mountains. A few [3]_____ thinkers like Pythagoras and Heraclides, far ahead of their time, developed glimmerings of the modern view, but their ideas fell into [4]_____ after Ptolemy systematized his geocentric theory in the second century A.D. Scientists then completely succumbed to the complacent belief that the earth was the center of the universe. They strenuously resisted change of any sort in that [5]_____.

Nicolaus Copernicus, a Polish-born astronomer of the sixteenth century, presented the [6]_____ suggestion that the center of our part of the universe was the sun, with the planets moving in circles around it. His [7]_____ led men like Brahe, Kepler, Galileo, and Newton on to [8]_____ the true nature of the system with its elliptically orbiting planets.

Through tiresome drudgery more and more facts have been learned about the universe. It is now clear that our solar system, with its sun, planets, and satellites, is but a minuscule part of the Milky Way, a galaxy that contains an [9]_____ horde of stars, some smaller than our sun with its diameter of 864,000 miles but many much larger. We see the universe as an aggregate of vast galaxies of suns, arranged in [10]_____ that may never be fully understood and will probably never be observed in their entirety.

EXERCISE 135:   For each numbered blank in Essay 15, provide the word or phrase which best completes the meaning of the sentence. Make your selection from the numbered groups, which correspond to the numbered blanks. These lists contain words that appeared in Essays 11 to 14.

1.	2.	3.	4.
cut down	variety	piscine	disrepute
forecast	challenge	serious	kernel
appealed	cog	mere	digest

5.	6.	7.	8.
hazard	clapping	speculation	sagging
relic	multiple	stress	exhibiting
notion	startling	bivalve	outliving

9.	10.
immense	quarters
avariciousness	summaries
adoptive	patterns

EXERCISE 136: Pronounce the following words, emphasizing the stressed syllable by saying the vowel louder, longer, and higher in pitch than the other vowels.

A.   Emphasize the first syllable of these words:

ages	systematized	system	challenge
heavenly	theory	orbiting	piscine
bodies	second	tiresome	serious
knowledge	century	drudgery	kernel
naturally	scientists	solar	hazard
interest	center	satellites	relic
greatly	strenuously	minuscule	notion
ancients	any	milky	clapping
universe	Polish	galaxy	multiple
valley	planets	smaller	startling
mountains	moving	many	bivalve
thinkers	circles	larger	sagging
glimmerings	Brahe	aggregate	quarters
modern	Kepler	never	summaries
after	Newton	fully	patterns
Ptolemy	nature	probably	

B. Emphasize the second syllable of these words:

astronomy	Pythagoras	astronomer	entirety
desire	ahead	presented	appealed
today's	developed	suggestion	variety
mechanical	ideas	around	exhibiting
devices	completely	elliptically	outliving
increased	succumbed	about	immense
depicted	complacent	contains	adoptive
essentially	belief	diameter	
conceived	resisted	arranged	
surrounded	Copernicus	observed	

C. Emphasize the third syllable of these words:

insurmountable	geocentric	Galileo	disrepute
Heraclides	Nicolaus	understood	speculation
avariciousness			

D. Emphasize the fourth syllable of this word:

imagination

EXERCISE 137: Read Essay 15 aloud with the blanks filled in.

EXERCISE 138: Be prepared to answer any questions that the teacher may ask on Essay 15.

EXERCISE 139: Give an oral summary of Essay 15.

EXERCISE 140: Write a summary of Essay 15.

EXERCISE 141: Write the parts of Essay 15 that the teacher dictates.

EXERCISE 142: Write a composition on a topic suggested by Essay 15.

EXERCISE 143: Answer the following questions, which contain words from Essays 11 to 15.

1. What language have you studied intensively?
2. Does a dictator have much power?
3. Would you call a king an ordinary person?
4. Does a school sometimes supply textbooks for the students?
5. Are people quiet when they have a scuffle?
6. Can freezing weather cause water pipes to burst?
7. When are peas more likely to be tender and sweet—when they are first picked or later?
8. Is the inner surface of your lip moist?
9. In which season would a person want to wear wool-lined shoes?
10. What is the name of the great current of warm water that moves eastward from North America to Europe?
11. Are umbrellas radially ribbed?
12. Can you gather fresh coconuts in this area?
13. Are the banks of a river usually muddy?
14. How many days a week do you have free of classes?
15. Is the growl of an angry dog mild?
16. Is it usually hard to pull a tooth after it has become loosened?
17. When do you see strollers in a park—on a clear day or a rainy one?
18. Is the job of learning English soon done?
19. What is the most delicious dessert you can think of?
20. Are you by no means hard-working?
21. Are there hundreds of seats in this room?
22. Does a talkative person pour out words?
23. Can you name some poets that have an enduring appeal?
24. What do you use to separate the skin of an apple from the pulp?
25. Which are sometimes flesh-colored—diamonds or pearls?
26. What can happen if you insert a finger into an electric light socket?
27. Do people have different views about smoking?
28. Do you think we have reached the ultimate in science yet?

29. Do most animals have a lifelong struggle for survival?
30. If a person dies of old age, do we say that he has been slain?
31. When you cried when you were young, did your mother some-times pop a piece of candy into your mouth to make you stop?
32. Would you be able to carry a bushel basket full of apples?
33. Does it take very little effort to build a house?
34. Do you like the gurgling sound that a baby makes when he is contented?
35. When somebody asks you a question, do you try to give him a proper answer?
36. Have you ever seen a piece of jewelry with a mother-of-pearl background?
37. What kinds of animals live at the bottom of the sea?
38. Which part of a pitcher is the lip?
39. Why do you suppose some people consider the heart to be the center of the emotions?
40. Is a cigarette less than a quarter of an inch in diameter?
41. Do you like chicken to be dipped in flour before it is fried?
42. How many cutting edges does a kitchen knife usually have?
43. When you were a child, did you ever get separated from your parents?
44. How long does it take to broil a steak?
45. Have you ever skated on a creek that had frozen?
46. Is a dog less than a third the size of a horse?

EXERCISE 144: Write an essay on one of the questions in Exercise 143.

ESSAY 16 SETTING IN POETRY
BY DEAN MORGAN SCHMITTER

It is a common observation that adults do not read poetry and that students do not, in general, have either any inclination for or appreciation of poetic art. Yet, there are some fervid few who do. The principal difference between the two groups is not that the latter has finer faculties but that it understands poetry. Somehow or other, most of us do not develop an understanding of how poetry works.

One of the ways poetry works is in the form of a little drama —that is, there is a character or characters, a setting, a subject under discussion, and an interpretation of or attitude toward the subject.

The second of these, the setting, may have so little intensity that it is brushed aside, often with no harm done for the practiced reader, who correctly appraises the situation. Such a reader is really using the apparently absent setting to turn his attention toward more intense elements; he is not ignoring it.

A poetic setting may vary from the mood-filled blankness of a Shakespearean sonnet to the sharp precision of Browning's upstairs gallery with the "last Duchess painted on the wall." Still, even the setting of a Shakespearean sonnet, though lacking in detail, is positive. It has subordinated detailed setting to thought—much as in a stage presentation a spotlight picks out an actor on a dark stage.

Other poems fall between the two extremes. Readers often pass over the setting of Shelley's "West Wind" ode; yet, their doing so fails to give the poem its due, for it is quite dramatic. The speaker—our dramatic character—is not speaking his lines in an unformed scene; he can best be understood by the reader's realizing where the poet has firmly placed him: in an autumn setting with the wind driving the sere leaves, "yellow, and black, and pale, and hectic red," and "the wingèd seeds" lying underfoot. The details are few, but they are enough. And, yes, the wind is out of the west.

Perhaps the picture of Keats' "Grecian Urn" is strong

enough so that no reader misses the finely described image. Nevertheless, the fully realized setting includes as well the speaker contemplating the urn as he speaks the lines of the poem. So does it in the same poet's "Ode to a Nightingale," and how many readers are sharply cognizant that a full reading of that poem includes awareness of a rural scene with what might be described as an offstage sound, the nightingale that "singest of summer in full-throated ease"?

The setting always deserves consideration, even when it is like a dark stage with no scenery. Its very absence may be part of the drama.

EXERCISE 145: Pronounce the following words, emphasizing the stressed syllable by saying the vowel louder, longer, and higher in pitch than the other vowels.

A. Emphasize the first syllable of these words:

setting	attitude	spotlight	finely
poetry	toward	actor	image
common	second	poem	fully
students	often	over	realized
general	practiced	Shelley's	contemplating
either	reader	doing	nightingale
any	really	speaker	money
fervid	using	speaking	sharply
principal	absent	realizing	cognizant
difference	elements	poet	reading
latter	vary	firmly	rural
finer	blankness	autumn	singest
faculties	sonnet	driving	summer
somehow	Browning's	yellow	throated
other	gallery	hectic	always
little	duchess	wingèd	scenery
drama	painted	lying	very
character	even	picture	absence
subject	lacking	Grecian	
under	positive	misses	

B. Emphasize the second syllable of these words:

between	appraise	Shakespearean	enough
develop	apparently	precision	perhaps
discussion	attention	subordinated	described
intensity	intense	extremes	includes
aside	ignoring	dramatic	awareness
correctly	poetic	unformed	deserves

C. Emphasize the third syllable of these words:

observation	understands	situation	understood
inclination	understanding	presentation	underfoot

D. Emphasize the fourth syllable of these words:

appreciation	nevertheless
interpretation	consideration

EXERCISE 146:   Read Essay 16 aloud.

EXERCISE 147:   Answer the following questions on the basis of Essay 16.

1. Do many adults read poetry?
2. How do students feel toward poetry?
3. How many people do read poetry?
4. Why do those people read it?
5. Why don't other people read poetry?
6. To what does the author compare a poem?
7. What are the ingredients of a drama?
8. Do poets sometimes omit reference to the setting?
9. How does the expert reader respond to the absence of a setting?
10. Are all settings the same?
11. What kind of setting do Shakespeare's sonnets have?
12. Is there much detail in the setting of Browning's "My Last Duchess"?
13. What analogy does the author use for Shakespeare's sonnets?

14. Do some readers disregard the setting of Shelley's "Ode to the West Wind"?
15. Why should they not do that?
16. What is the setting of the west-wind ode?
17. What are some of the details that are mentioned?
18. Is Keats explicit about the Grecian urn?
19. What, besides the urn, is the setting of that ode?
20. Is the speaker also a part of "Ode to a Nightingale"?
21. Where is the scene laid in that poem?
22. What sound is a part of its setting?
23. Should the setting of a poem ever be ignored?
24. Can you pick out two words in the essay which are used more often in poetry than in ordinary conversation?

EXERCISE 148: Give an oral summary of Essay 16.

EXERCISE 149: Write a summary of Essay 16.

EXERCISE 150: Write the parts of Essay 16 that the teacher dictates.

EXERCISE 151: Write a composition on a topic suggested by Essay 16.

EXERCISE 152: Answer the following questions, which contain words from Essay 16.

1. If you wrote a poem about this room, what would be parts of the setting?
2. When a person is very angry, does his speech usually express little intensity?
3. Is a map which is lacking in detail as serviceable as it could be?
4. With which holiday are the colors yellow and black associated, do you know?

5. Is a poet using a figure of speech when he calls a star "an eye of heaven"?
6. Is the urge to survive so strong that most of us want to go on living somehow or other?
7. Which aims at creating a mood in the reader—a horror story or a chemistry textbook?
8. Is a wife happy if her husband passes over their wedding anniversary?
9. Does it take much skill to etch an image on glass?
10. Is an epigram a witty observation?
11. Is any harm done if a person walks on newly planted grass?
12. When a person joins a group, does he sometimes have to subordinate his desires to those of the group?
13. Are hospitals customarily painted in hectic colors?
14. Does the very thought of war make you shudder?
15. For the sake of politeness, is it a good idea to put a command into the form of a question?
16. Which would you more likely think of as a blankness—a mountainous area or a desert?
17. Is a rescue just in the nick of time quite dramatic?
18. Where do people contemplate paintings?
19. Does a practiced political speaker decide on his statements before or after he appraises his audience?
20. Who is your favorite Shakespearean character?
21. In which part of the world would you find snow lying underfoot in July?
22. Do you see many nightingales in this area?
23. Is life apparently absent on most of the planets?
24. How many lines does a sonnet have?
25. Is the scene in a nightmare usually unformed?
26. Is it easy to turn a child's attention toward financial matters?
27. Do you expect a bus driver to be sharply cognizant of traffic when he is on duty?
28. Why is a spotlight usually directed toward the principal actor on a stage?
29. When is the wind here more likely to be cold—when it is out of the north or out of the south?
30. Do you think that a teacher would like to have fervid students?
31. What do you expect to see in an art gallery?

32. In which season do leaves become sere?

33. Which is usually an offstage sound—a telephone ring or a knock on a door?

34. What is the principal difference between the government of France and that of England?

35. Do the police have more trouble with some elements of society than with others?

36. Which is more likely to be subjective—a diary or a weather report?

37. Would a full-throated cry be loud or soft?

38. What sort of attitude do you have toward pets?

39. How do you feel in a room that lacks warmth?

40. Which month falls between June and July?

EXERCISE 153: Write an essay on one of the questions in Exercise 152.

ESSAY 17 APOLLO

One of the chief gods of the Greek and, later, Roman pantheon, Phoebus Apollo, the mighty protector from [1]_____,
seems to have been originally a [2]_____ deity, like his twin
sister Artemis (or Diana), since the earliest references to him
are in connection with shepherds and beekeepers. Just as his
sister was associated with the moon, Apollo came to represent
the light- and life-giving qualities, as well as the deadly power,
of the sun, and it became [3]_____ later to identify him with
the sun god Helios. Leader of the Muses, he was the patron of
music and poetic art; by some he was accounted the father of
Orpheus, the celebrated bard whose tragic love for Eurydice
has been a favored [4]_____ for numberless playwrights. All-
seeing, Apollo was the master of prophecy, and the oracle at
Delphi grew famous for its [5]_____ of the god's omens. On
Cassandra he bestowed the gift of predicting the future, but
when she spurned his advances, he placed a curse on her: People henceforth [6]_____ her auguries. To his son Aesculapius
he passed on the [7]_____ for healing, and to his half brother
Hermes he presented the caduceus, the [8]_____ staff now
the symbol of medicine. A great number of magnificent statues
of Apollo have been preserved from classical times, and his
[9]_____ appears on many ancient Greek and Roman
[10]_____.

EXERCISE 154:   For each numbered blank in Essay 17, provide the word
or phrase which best completes the meaning of the sentence. Make
your selection from the numbered groups, which correspond to the
numbered blanks. These lists contain words that appeared in Essay 16.

1.	2.	3.	4.
harm	rural	sere	intensity
setting	fervid	intense	subject
sonnet	unformed	common	duchess

5.	6.	7.	8.
attitude	smelted	spotlight	winged
interpretation	ignored	faculty	in-law
inclination	plunged	blankness	underfoot

9.	10.
image	moods
element	urns
precision	dues

EXERCISE 155: Pronounce the following words, emphasizing the stressed syllable by saying the vowel louder, longer, and higher in pitch than the other vowels.

A. Emphasize the first syllable of these words:

later	Helios	Delphi	setting
Roman	leader	famous	sonnet
pantheon	Muses	omens	rural
Phoebus	patron	future	fervid
mighty	music	people	common
deity	father	henceforth	subject
sister	Orpheus	auguries	duchess
Artemis	celebrated	healing	attitude
earliest	tragic	brother	smelted
references	favored	Hermes	spotlight
shepherds	numberless	symbol	faculty
beekeepers	playwrights	medicine	blankness
giving	seeing	statues	image
qualities	master	classical	element
deadly	prophecy	many	
power	oracle	ancient	

B. Emphasize the second syllable of these words:

Apollo	identify	advances	intense
protector	poetic	presented	intensity
originally	accounted	caduceus	ignored
Diana	Eurydice	magnificent	precision
connection	Cassandra	preserved	
associated	bestowed	appears	
became	predicting	unformed	

C. Emphasize the third syllable of these words:

represent   Aesculapius   inclination   underfoot

D. Emphasize the fourth syllable of this word:

interpretation

EXERCISE 156: Read Essay 17 aloud with the blanks filled in.

EXERCISE 157: Be prepared to answer any questions on Essay 17 that the teacher may ask.

EXERCISE 158: Give an oral summary of Essay 17.

EXERCISE 159: Write a summary of Essay 17.

EXERCISE 160: Write the parts of Essay 17 that the teacher dictates.

EXERCISE 161: Write a composition on a topic suggested by Essay 17.

EXERCISE 162: Answer the following questions, which contain words from Essays 16 and 17.

1. Do you have any inclination to travel widely?
2. Does the effectiveness of a play depend greatly on the ability of the actors to speak their lines?
3. What is the setting of Tolstoy's *War and Peace?*
4. Is Paris a rural area?
5. To what kind of store would you go to buy an urn?
6. Do you think you have finer faculties than an imbecile?
7. How much does the temperature usually vary in twenty-four hours in this area?
8. Are accidents very common on the highways?
9. What is your opinion of a person who brushes his obligations aside?
10. When a doctor gives you a diagnostic test to see if you have a particular disease, do you hope that the result will be positive or negative?
11. Did you know that some brightly colored fish become pale when they are frightened?
12. Does the scenery add much to your enjoyment of a play?
13. Have you yet developed an understanding of how radio works?
14. Is a patent intended to give an inventor his due?
15. Do you believe you use your abilities fully?
16. Are you a practiced violinist?
17. In which would you probably find more thought—in an essay written by a cowboy or one by a philosopher?
18. What can a winged seed do that most other seeds cannot?
19. Would you say that a person had to develop an appreciation of classical music?
20. Is a bucket much the same as a pail?
21. Do you feel you have any poetic ability?
22. Who are some characters of Shakespeare's with whom you are familiar?
23. Which would be more concerned with details—an accountant or a house painter?
24. Is an actor's use of his hands part of his dramatic art?
25. Is a photographer particularly concerned about the precision of his lenses?

26. Does an architect designing an auditorium give much thought to placing the stage so that speakers can best be understood?

27. What is the customary subject under discussion at a bankers' meeting?

28. Would you probably be able to pick out a rose in a mixed bouquet?

29. Did the Roman Empire antedate the Grecian?

30. Would a teacher like his students to have intense concentration on their studies?

31. What word do we use to describe a statement that has two possible interpretations?

32. Do you think you will be here next autumn?

33. In an argument between liberals and conservatives, would you side with the latter?

34. Do you try to ignore people whom you do not like?

35. If the North and South Poles have one extreme of temperature, which part of the earth has the other extreme?

36. Is instant coffee finely or coarsely ground?

37. Do you enjoy an anxiety-filled period?

38. What would you say is the principal difference between a drama and a short story?

39. What do you call the husband of a duchess?

40. Have you ever seen a stage presentation of *Faust?*

EXERCISE 163:   Write an essay on one of the questions in Exercise 162.

ESSAY 18 "SWEET LORRAINE"

BY THOMAS R. GOETHALS

The curious tricks the mind seems to delight in playing upon us and even upon itself are a source of constant wonder to me. So simple do they seem that we often forget them—if, indeed, we have been aware of their happening at all; but every now and then, as if it were laughing at us, the mind startles us with a trick we can neither quite forget nor fully explain. Such was my experience one night not long ago. While I was preparing a solitary dinner, accompanied only by the radio playing softly in the background (how good it is to hear the human voice after a long day of reading!), suddenly, as if from the very act of placing the hamburgers into the hot pan, there flashed before me a scene long forgotten, isolated, and yet perfectly framed. Perhaps even the hamburgers ceased sizzling while I wondered at that scene in my mind's eye and, possibly even then, groped to find what it was in the deep, dim past that such a scene had stood for and why I should have remembered it with detail and impact.

It is not a memorable scene, surely not from the artistic point of view of color and composition, of perspective and design. There is simply a tavern on a street corner somewhere in Europe. There the brown building stands in the early, rainy spring evening, its narrow, peaked gables and fretted windows reminiscent of the fairy tales we used to read as children. Across the street, at the same intersection, crouches a long, low building, obscured by dusk and rain falling, and from above the two buildings the street itself descends a long hill. The street is made of cobblestones, wet and flecked with straw, and it is different from streets in Paris or Hong Kong or Buenos Aires, and there I am on the corner, thinking that if there is a difference in streets, not merely in the material but in the very quality of streets, how much more might I be moved by differences other than those of streets in the rain, differences that soldiers do not often have the time or inclination to distinguish, much less notice, so quickly do they move on from one city to another in time of war.

I was a soldier then, and I had just come out of that tavern, recently requisitioned for a mess hall, and I was standing there in the rain, smoking and thinking that because I was a soldier in that town where the cobbled street ran down the hill, there really *was* a difference, and the civilian who abruptly scurried across the street and disappeared into the drizzle might never know how important to me he became simply in the act of crossing my strange street, which for him might be shabby with familiarity and despair. It was the fragility of the moment, the tension in mood and tone, caught, without warning, in a moment of peace amid a world at war, that evoked my emotional response, colored my perceptions—a moment heightened, perhaps, by the fatigue of a long day's journey by jeep, by the relaxation of a good meal (hamburgers, do you suppose?) inside the tavern with fellow soldiers, who had been friendly and bawdy and homesick—and it had all led to that moment of standing on a street corner, alone, in the rain, and was even then, from the sound of motors on the hill, to lead to more. A convoy of trucks filed past my corner, and I caught a glimpse of the insignia on the bumpers, the white cross of Lorraine on a blue shield.

Right then I stopped remembering, quickly turned down the gas below the smoking hamburgers, and instinctively paused, listening, listening to music from the radio—a singer crooning an old favorite, "Sweet Lorraine"—and then, as I began to understand, listening to my mind maliciously asking why that scene remained so clear to me in its obscurity.

EXERCISE 164: Pronounce the following words, emphasizing the stressed syllable by saying the vowel louder, longer, and higher in pitch than the other vowels.

A. Emphasize the first syllable of these words:

curious	hamburgers	fairy	crossing
playing	into	children	shabby
even	isolated	crouches	moment
constant	perfectly	falling	tension
wonder	sizzling	cobblestones	warning
often	wondered	different	colored
happening	possibly	thinking	heightened
every	impact	difference	journey
laughing	memorable	merely	fellow
startles	surely	quality	friendly
neither	color	other	bawdy
fully	simply	soldiers	homesick
solitary	tavern	notice	motors
dinner	corner	quickly	convoy
only	somewhere	city	bumpers
radio	Europe	recently	listening
softly	building	standing	music
background	early	smoking	singer
human	rainy	cobbled	crooning
after	evening	really	favorite
reading	narrow	scurried	asking
suddenly	gables	drizzle	
very	fretted	never	
placing	windows	simply	

B. Emphasize the second syllable of these words:

Lorraine	forgotten	because	fatigue
delight	perhaps	civilian	suppose
upon	remembered	abruptly	inside
itself	artistic	important	alone
forget	perspective	became	insignia
indeed	design	despair	remembering
aware	across	fragility	below
explain	obscured	without	instinctively
experience	above	amid	began
ago	descends	evoked	maliciously
preparing	material	emotional	remained

accompanied	distinguish	response	obscurity
before	another	perceptions	

C. Emphasize the third syllable of these words:

composition	intersection	requisitioned	relaxation
reminiscent	inclination	disappeared	understand

D. Emphasize the fourth syllable of this word:

familiarity

EXERCISE 165: Read Essay 18 aloud.

EXERCISE 166: Answer the following questions on the basis of Essay 18.

1. What ability of the mind fascinates the author?
2. Do the deceptions appear to be complicated?
3. Do we usually remember the tricks?
4. What was the author doing at the time of the essay?
5. Was anyone with him?
6. Was the kitchen silent?
7. What had the author been doing previously that day?
8. What was he cooking?
9. Had he thought of the scene recently?
10. Did he remember it clearly?
11. Did the author become oblivious of his present surroundings?
12. Did he try to find a connection between the scene and something else?
13. Does he think that the scene is notable?
14. What is the dominant building in it?
15. Which part of the street does the building occupy?
16. Where is the scene?
17. What color is the building?
18. What time of day is it?
19. Which season is it?
20. Is the weather clear?

21. Is the roof of the building flat?
22. Are the windows plain in design?
23. What do they remind the author of?
24. Are there any other buildings in the scene?
25. What is the terrain of the scene?
26. Is the street paved with concrete?
27. Is the street bare?
28. Does the author think the street is similar to those in other cities?
29. What thought does the street prompt in him?
30. Does he believe that cultural differences are likely to impress soldiers?
31. What was the author's occupation at that time?
32. Where had he been?
33. What was the tavern being used for?
34. What was the author doing on the street?
35. Why did he decide that there was a difference in the quality of streets?
36. Why did the noncombatant become important to the author?
37. Did the civilian know the effect he had on the author?
38. How did the civilian probably feel about the street?
39. Was a war going on at that time?
40. What were some of the factors that influenced the author's thinking at that moment?
41. Had the author been in the town all day?
42. Was he tired?
43. Had he eaten well?
44. With whom had he eaten?
45. How had his companions acted?
46. What passed the corner?
47. What was on the bumpers?
48. What was the design?
49. What action did the author make then?
50. Were the hamburgers cool?
51. What did the author hear on the radio?
52. In what manner was the singer singing?
53. What connection did the song have with the author's previous thoughts?
54. What did he ask himself?

EXERCISE 167: Give an oral summary of Essay 18.

EXERCISE 168: Write a summary of Essay 18.

EXERCISE 169: Write the parts of Essay 18 that the teacher dictates.

EXERCISE 170: Write a composition on a topic suggested by Essay 18.

EXERCISE 171: Answer the following questions, which contain words from Essay 18.

1. Does it snow in this city every now and then?
2. Do you enjoy the tricks that a magician plays upon his audience?
3. Can you see your childhood home in your mind's eye right now?
4. What does a person purchase at a tavern?
5. Are hamburgers popular in this country?
6. When you are taking an examination, do you feel happy when you have to grope to find the answers to some of the questions?
7. Would you picture the Sphinx as crouching on the landscape?
8. Does perspective determine the size of objects in a painting?
9. What often obscures your view when you are up in an airplane?
10. While you were thinking about something else, has a scene from your childhood ever flashed before you?
11. When does dusk come these days?
12. Did the launching of the first earth satellite have much impact upon people's imagination?
13. Is it tiring to walk on a street made of cobblestones?
14. Which sizzles on a stove—boiling cabbage or frying meat?
15. Does a flight of wild geese make a memorable scene?
16. Does this building have a peaked roof?
17. When would a horse be flecked with sweat—after he had been grazing or after he had been racing?

18. Are windows in modern buildings usually fretted?
19. Which would rustle—a mattress filled with cotton or one stuffed with straw?
20. Which will get you wetter—a downpour or a drizzle?
21. Do you feel that some restaurants have a better tone than others?
22. Do you like to be caught at times by a feeling of complete well-being?
23. When were shields customarily carried by soldiers?
24. Do opera singers habitually croon?
25. Why do ships travel in convoys during wartime?
26. Do you know a flag that has blue on white?
27. Which would probably requisition a building—an architect or an army officer?
28. Is much freight carried by trucks in this country?
29. If a teacher asked you to stop whispering, would you cease right then?
30. How long does it sometimes take for a string of freight cars to file past a given point?
31. Do you agree with the proverb "Familiarity breeds contempt"?
32. Do you make it a practice to tell bawdy jokes at social gatherings?
33. Does the gas usually burn above the racks in an oven?
34. What is your opinion of a person who asks you questions maliciously?
35. What purpose does an insignia serve?
36. Is most glassware characterized by fragility?
37. What is sometimes affixed to a car's bumpers?
38. Are a person's prejudices likely to color his perceptions?
39. Have you ever seen insects scurry across a kitchen floor when you suddenly turned on a light?
40. Do you feel fine when you are in despair?

EXERCISE 172: Write an essay on one of the questions in Exercise 171.

ESSAY 19 THE STATUE OF LIBERTY

Passengers arriving in New York by ship enjoy an advantage over those flying in by plane: They have the [1]_____ of the end of their journey [2]_____ by the imposing sight of the Statue of Liberty looming above them. Probably no other national monument in the United States [3]_____ as keen an emotional [4]_____ in its viewers as does that colossal symbol of freedom. Soldiers and [5]_____, visitors and [6]_____ citizens—all acknowledge the excitement that is aroused in them as they [7]_____ their first [8]_____ of that gigantic figure.

As impressive as the statue is its history. Late in the past century, the project was proposed to commemorate the French and American Revolutions, and funds were publicly raised, chiefly by small donations, in France and the United States. Active in soliciting contributions was Joseph Pulitzer, the newspaper owner who later endowed the Pulitzer prizes for meritorious work in journalism and literature. One supporter who never seemed to [9]_____ in his furthering of the project was its designer, the Alsatian sculptor F. A. Bartholdi (his mother is reputed to have served as the model for the statue), who was himself for a time a refugee in New York. Gustave Eiffel, whose name endures in the Eiffel Tower in Paris, aided in the execution of the design. The statue was constructed in France, shipped to the United States in sections, and erected on Bedloe's Island, whose first owner had fled from religious persecution in France. The name of the island was changed by an [10]_____ of Congress in 1956 to Liberty Island.

EXERCISE 173:   For each numbered blank in Essay 19, provide the word or phrase which best completes the meaning of the sentence. Make your selection from the numbered groups, which correspond to the numbered blanks. These lists contain words that appeared in Essay 18.

1.	2.	3.	4.
tension	cobbled	evokes	response
drizzle	filed	scurries	tavern
jeep	heightened	croons	bumper

5.	6.	7.	8.
convoys	homesick	catch	mess
civilians	instinctive	turn down	requisition
familiarities	malicious	skimp	glimpse

9.	10.
clarify	act
pause	insignia
blot up	apricot

EXERCISE 174: Pronounce the following words, emphasizing the stressed syllable by saying the vowel louder, longer, and higher in pitch than the other vowels.

A. Emphasize the first syllable of these words:

statue	visitors	journalism	congress
liberty	citizens	literature	tension
passengers	figure	never	drizzle
over	history	furthering	cobbled
flying	century	sculptor	filed
journey	project	mother	heightened
looming	publicly	model	scurries
probably	chiefly	refugee	tavern
other	active	Eiffel	bumper
national	Joseph	tower	homesick
monument	Pulitzer	Paris	clarify
viewers	newspaper	aided	apricot
symbol	owner	sections	
freedom	later	Bedloe's	
soldiers	prizes	island	

B. Emphasize the second syllable of these words:

arriving	aroused	designer	religious
enjoy	gigantic	Alsatian	evokes
advantage	impressive	Bartholdi	response
imposing	proposed	reputed	civilians
above	commemorate	himself	instinctive
united	American	Gustave	malicious
emotional	donations	endures	insignia
colossal	soliciting	design	
acknowledge	endowed	constructed	
excitement	supporter	erected	

C. Emphasize the third syllable of these words:

revolutions	meritorious	persecution
contributions	execution	requisition

D. Emphasize the fourth syllable of this word:

familiarities

EXERCISE 175: Read Essay 19 aloud with the blanks filled in.

EXERCISE 176: Be prepared to answer any questions on Essay 19 that the teacher may ask.

EXERCISE 177: Give an oral summary of Essay 19.

EXERCISE 178: Write a summary of Essay 19.

EXERCISE 179: Write the parts of Essay 19 that the teacher dictates.

EXERCISE 180: Write a composition on a topic suggested by Essay 19.

EXERCISE 181: Answer the following questions, which contain words from Essays 18 and 19.

1. Have you ever seen a soldier?
2. Do most students have a feeling of tension before an examination, would you say?
3. What are some of the emotional responses that a human being is capable of?
4. What is the only sure remedy when you are homesick?
5. Do certain sights evoke memories of your childhood?
6. When is a person not a civilian?
7. Would you probably be able to identify a man later if you had merely caught a glimpse of him before?
8. If you are planning to buy a carpet, do you give much thought to its design?
9. When you go to a zoo, do you expect to find curious animals?
10. Do you ever wonder at the current women's fashions?
11. Do home appliances made by different companies differ not merely in material but also in craftsmanship?
12. When you are exhausted, does the very thought of moving make you wince?
13. Should a student be concerned about the quality of the instruction he receives?
14. Are there any physical phenomena that no one has fully explained?
15. Is a self-centered person likely to be moved by the troubles of other people?
16. Do you still remember any of the fairy tales you heard when you were a child?
17. Would you say that the invention of the wheel took place in the deep, dim past?
18. Would you see a doctor if you had a constant headache?
19. What does the movement of your head from right to left and back again stand for?
20. Is a phonetician sometimes able to distinguish sounds that seem alike to a layman?
21. How many people go with you when you take a solitary walk?
22. Which is usually narrower—an avenue or an alley?
23. Do you prepare your own meals?

24. Which is the faster way of descending a long hill—by foot or by bicycle?
25. Are you aware of the movement of the earth through space?
26. Is a scene perfectly framed if some of the details are lacking?
27. Is snow likely to accumulate on houses with gables?
28. When a student is very tired, does it ever seem to him as if his textbook were laughing at him?
29. Have you ever imagined what your life would be like if you never forgot anything at all?
30. What would you suspect if a car suddenly ceased running?
31. Do you feel fatigue at the end of the day?
32. What kind of mood are you in after you have read a very tragic story?
33. Have you just come into this room?
34. How much distance can a person cover in a day's journey by bicycle?
35. Are there any taverns near here?
36. Does the average housewife like her husband to bring guests home without warning?
37. What song is your favorite?
38. Is the equivalent of the word *sweet* in your language used as a term of endearment?
39. Is it a good idea to wear shabby clothes to an interview for a professional position?
40. Do you ever listen to your conscience?

EXERCISE 182: Write an essay on one of the questions in Exercise 181.

ESSAY 20 PUNS

A *pun* or *play on words* or *paronomasia* is the use of words or phrases to convey a "double meaning." It involves words which have identical or similar pronunciations but diverse meanings. For example, since the word *can* means not only "be able" but also "preserve," there is a pun in "We eat all the fruit we can, and what we can't we can." Speakers of a great many languages, if not all, [1]_____ in punning. A well-known German pun relies on the identicalness of pronunciation of *ist* ("is") and *iszt* ("eats"): When spoken, the sentence *Man ist was man ist* may be interpreted to mean either "One is what one is" or "One is what one eats." The basis of the founding of the Catholic Church is a [2]_____ pun: In the Greek version of the Bible, Christ says to his disciple Peter, whom Roman Catholics regard as the first Pope, "Thou art Peter [*Petros*], and upon this rock [*Petra*] I will build my church."

An effective pun makes an [3]_____ by revealing a [4]_____ relationship between ideas and is, therefore, often employed in [5]_____ or philosophic works. For instance, to appreciate Shakespeare [6]_____, one must be [7]_____ of his multifarious puns. However, since in the popular mind the word *pun* has come to mean solely a [8]_____ of humor or an expression of lighthearted exuberance, other terms are used to [9]_____ the device in its serious employment. The word *ambiguity* has recently gained currency in literary criticism, but its defect is that it can also [10]_____ a lack of clarity, either intentional or unintentional.

EXERCISE 183: For each numbered blank in Essay 20, provide the word or phrase which best completes the meaning of the sentence. Make your selection from the numbered groups, which correspond to the numbered blanks. These lists contain words that appeared in Essays 16 to 19.

1.	2.	3.	4.
fleck	peaked	impact	groping
delight	reminiscent	intersection	startling
frame	memorable	inclination	crouching

5.	6.	7.	8.
artistic	fully	fretted	source
cobblestone	dimly	aware	pan
constant	merely	solitary	tavern

9.	10.
cease	come about
wonder	stand for
distinguish	sizzle

EXERCISE 184: Pronounce the following words, emphasizing the stressed syllable by saying the vowel louder, longer, and higher in pitch than the other vowels.

A. Emphasize the first syllable of these words:

phrases	sentence	popular	groping
double	either	solely	startling
meaning	basis	humor	crouching
similar	founding	hearted	cobblestone
only	Catholic	other	constant
able	version	serious	fully
also	Bible	recently	dimly
speakers	Peter	currency	merely
many	Roman	literary	fretted
languages	therefore	criticism	solitary
punning	often	clarity	tavern
German	instance	memorable	wonder
spoken	Shakespeare	impact	sizzle

B. Emphasize the second syllable of these words:

convey	interpreted	ideas	intentional
involves	disciple	employed	delight
identical	regard	appreciate	artistic
diverse	upon	however	aware
example	effective	expression	distinguish
preserve	revealing	exuberance	about
relies	relationship	device	
identicalness	between	employment	

C. Emphasize the third syllable of these words:

philosophic	ambiguity	reminiscent	inclination
multifarious	unintentional	intersection	

D. Emphasize the fourth syllable of these words:

paronomasia   pronunciation

EXERCISE 185: Read Essay 20 aloud with the blanks filled in.

EXERCISE 186: Be prepared to answer any questions on Essay 20 that the teacher may ask.

EXERCISE 187: Give an oral summary of Essay 20.

EXERCISE 188: Write a summary of Essay 20.

EXERCISE 189: Write the parts of Essay 20 that the teacher dictates.

EXERCISE 190: Write a composition on a topic suggested by Essay 20.

EXERCISE 191: Answer the following questions, which contain words from Essays 16 to 20.

1. Is spring usually rainy here?
2. Is the circulation of blood a source of wonder to you?
3. Have you ever come upon an old letter that recalled a friend long forgotten?
4. Does the composition of body tissues seem simple to you?
5. Is it better to learn isolated words or words in context?
6. Is there a tendency to have inflation in time of war?
7. Do you fry eggs in a hot or cool pan?
8. Would a zoologist probably have the inclination to investigate an offspring that had characteristics different from those of its parents?
9. Do you become annoyed when you cannot quite remember a person's name?
10. Do many housewives do their chores accompanied by the radio?
11. Which would probably look on an incident from an artistic point of view—a policeman or a painter?
12. What do you like to do after a long day of working?
13. Which would more likely be expected to move on shortly—an itinerant worker or a medical doctor?
14. Do love scenes in the movies usually have music playing softly in the background?
15. After a course in painting, would you be likely to become more aware of the composition of a picture?
16. Does the motor of a speedboat usually make a lot of noise?
17. How long does it take an airplane in the sky to disappear from sight?
18. Can you learn a language simply by listening to people speak it?
19. Can you see farther from a hill than from a mountain?
20. What would the police do to you if they found you in the act of robbing a bank?
21. Which could travel over hilly terrain better—a taxi or a jeep?
22. When does a mother of several small children have a moment of peace?
23. What is your favorite means of relaxation?

24. What should you do before crossing a street?
25. When was the last time that this country was at war?
26. Does life seem worth living after a good meal?
27. If you want to cook something quickly, do you turn the gas down?
28. Would a wagon probably make much noise on a cobbled street?
29. Would it be a good idea to use your fingers to pick up a smoking piece of meat?
30. Has your mind ever asked you why you did a certain thing?
31. What can happen if you abruptly stop a car?
32. Can a lie lead to a lot of trouble?
33. Do you instinctively blink your eyes when someone turns on a bright light?
34. Do you often recall scenes of your childhood?
35. Do idle young men here have the habit of standing on street corners?
36. Why does a speaker pause when his audience applauds one of his statements?
37. Does the plot of a story always remain clear to you even years later?
38. Do you like to hear a human voice after you have been by yourself for a long time?
39. Have you read a fairy tale recently?
40. Did anyone ever startle you by coming up behind you and making a loud noise?
41. How many streets usually come together at an intersection?
42. Do most children seem to delight in making up impossible stories?
43. Do you often see a person giving out handbills on a street corner in this city?
44. What is the primary source of energy for the earth?

EXERCISE 192: Write an essay on one of the questions in Exercise 191.

ESSAY 21 A LETTER OF COMPLAINT

BY CLIFFORD C. NELSON

754 West End Avenue
Round Valley, N.Y.
March 30, 19___

Manager
Snyder's Department Store
New York 5, N.Y.

Dear Sir:

For a number of years my wife and I have been dealing with
Snyder's and have bought several home appliances as well as
other merchandise. I have a Snyder's charge account, which I
have used a great deal, as your records will show. My son runs
in Snyder's sneakers; my small daughters run in and out of
Snyder's rompers. My walls are painted with Snyder's One-
Coat Satin Paint. My lawn is mowed with a Snyder's gas-
powered motor; my clothes washed in a Snyder's Handy
Spindri; my hamburgers done in the backyard in summer on
a Snyder's mobile barbecue pit. In short, much of what I have
has been yours.

Until now the service on all this stuff has been, if somewhat
grumpy here and there, at least adequate. That is why I am
shocked and hurt at the treatment we have been receiving
recently at the rather heavy hands of your installation men,
who, frankly, have been beating the stuffing out of the gas
range I bought two weeks ago. The installation—or lack of it—
has been based on incompetence or indifference or both. Apparently none of the "service" men seems to know or care very
much about getting the range in properly or taking the necessary safety precautions—with the result that much of the work

that ought to have been done by Snyder's has been thrust off on the Town Service people, who, I can assure you, are getting weary of adjusting a range sold by a competitor. There have been gas bubbles and outright leaks, and this morning, after another so-called repair visit by one of your men, the house was filled with gas fumes—to the fatigue of my mother-in-law, not to mention the kindergarten canary that is boarding with us during Easter vacation. We were saved only through the fortunate presence of a house painter, who shut off the main inlet because "I didn't want the house to go to heaven and me not get paid."

If this negligence had been the work of an arrogant fly-by-night outfit doing me a "favor," I could make an extra charge to experience and forget it, but when a reliable organization like Snyder's bills me for an installation which never seems finished and causes me great inconvenience and near grief, something is remiss somewhere. Living as I do on the psychic reward which at my company passes for a salary, I can ill afford it.

I thought that as manager you would want to know all this.

Sincerely yours,

Robert Crumbleton

EXERCISE 193: Pronounce the following words, emphasizing the stressed syllable by saying the vowel louder, longer, and higher in pitch than the other vowels.

A. Emphasize the first syllable of these words:

letter	mobile	people	heaven
valley	barbecue	weary	negligence
manager	service	bubbles	arrogant
Snyder's	somewhat	outright	outfit

number	grumpy	morning	doing
dealing	adequate	after	favor
several	treatment	visit	extra
other	recently	mother	never
merchandise	rather	mention	finished
records	heavy	kindergarten	causes
sneakers	frankly	boarding	something
daughters	beating	during	somewhere
rompers	stuffing	Easter	living
painted	very	fortunate	psychic
satin	getting	only	company
powered	properly	presence	passes
motor	taking	painter	salary
hamburgers	necessary	inlet	Robert
summer	safety	didn't	Crumbleton

B. Emphasize the second syllable of these words:

complaint	indifference	another	reliable
department	apparently	repair	remiss
backyard	about	fatigue	reward
appliances	precautions	canary	afford
account	result	vacation	sincerely
until	assure	because	
receiving	adjusting	experience	
incompetence	competitor	forget	

C. Emphasize the third syllable of these words:

installation   inconvenience

D. Emphasize the fourth syllable of this word:

organization

EXERCISE 194: Read Essay 21 aloud.

EXERCISE 195: Answer the following questions on the basis of Essay 21.

1. To whom is the letter addressed?
2. How long has Mr. Crumbleton been buying from Snyder's?
3. Has he bought very much from the store?
4. Does he pay cash for his purchases?
5. What does he buy for his son?
6. What does Mr. Crumbleton buy for his daughters?
7. What has he used Snyder's paint for?
8. How does he mow his grass?
9. What is washed in the washing machine?
10. Where and when does he use his movable barbecue stove?
11. Did many of Mr. Crumbleton's belongings come from the department store?
12. Has the company taken care of most of the equipment?
13. How does Mr. Crumbleton feel about the most recent service?
14. Have the servicemen been careful with the stove?
15. Have they installed it correctly?
16. Do the servicemen seem very competent?
17. Have some other people had to do the work that Snyder's was supposed to do?
18. Are those people glad to do that work?
19. Has any gas escaped from the stove?
20. What was the effect on the mother-in-law?
21. Why is there a bird in the house?
22. Who turned off the gas?
23. Why didn't he want the house to explode?
24. Would Mr. Crumbleton expect such carelessness from an unreliable company?
25. Is he surprised at Snyder's action?
26. Is Mr. Crumbleton well-to-do?
27. Can you detect any puns in Essay 21?

EXERCISE 196: Give an oral summary of Essay 21.

EXERCISE 197: Write a summary of Essay 21.

EXERCISE 198: Write the parts of Essay 21 that the teacher dictates.

EXERCISE 199: Write a composition on a topic suggested by Essay 21.

EXERCISE 200: Answer the following questions, which contain words from Essay 21.

1. Have you ever written a letter of complaint to a company?
2. What is the difference between a charge account and an installment plan?
3. Do you like to be waited on by a grumpy "clerk"?
4. When a person says he is going to "beat the stuffing out of" something, is he using figurative language?
5. Do you like to buy from a company that is remiss in the conduct of its business?
6. Is approval by other people a psychic reward for effort?
7. Is a manager the person immediately responsible for the operation of a store?
8. Can some counterfeit money pass for legal money?
9. Is a department store a small shop?
10. Have you ever seen a machine that could spin wet clothes around until they were dry?
11. Can you cook more than one thing at a time on a range?
12. When you apologize to someone and he says, "Forget it," does he mean that he accepts your apology?
13. Would you wear sneakers to a formal party?
14. Does a lazy man try to thrust work off on other people?
15. When might a person say that his house went to heaven?
16. Have you ever bought anything that you could ill afford?
17. Do people who live in an apartment usually have a backyard?
18. Do rompers cover the legs entirely?
19. Is a wagon a mobile vehicle?
20. How old are children who go to kindergarten?
21. Why are new walls often given two coats of paint?
22. When you barbecue meat, do you fry it or roast it?
23. Why do some people keep canaries in their homes?
24. Do you like to associate with an arrogant person?

25. How does satin feel?
26. Is a well a kind of pit?
27. Do you think of an unskilled person as having heavy hands?
28. Would you want to buy stock in a fly-by-night company?
29. Do you feel disturbed after a near accident?
30. When a person says "In short," is he going to make a summary or a detailed analysis?
31. Have you ever seen an outfit repairing roads?
32. Why do homeowners mow their lawns?
33. If a gas range is not got in properly, what may happen?
34. Do you express admiration when you say that a person is a "so-called authority"?
35. Does a complicated machine usually need service from time to time?
36. Will all faucets stop operating if you shut off the main inlet for water in a building?
37. Why does a department store want to be considered a reliable organization?
38. Is the climate in this area frequently unpleasant, not to mention unpredictable?
39. Have you ever been billed for a purchase you did not make?
40. What is your opinion of a person who tells outright lies?

EXERCISE 201: Write an essay on one of the questions in Exercise 200.

ESSAY 22 SAFETY

The endeavor to ensure safety has become a hallmark of the present century. Large businesses have come to realize that they can ill [1]_____ the loss in efficiency that an attitude of [2]_____ can cause. Moreover, both they and insurance companies are concerned with safety [3]_____ in order to decrease the cost of workmen's compensation and litigation over [4]_____, not to mention the loss of business to competitors through charges of [5]_____. Humanitarianism and growth of social consciousness have been other factors in the safety movement. Tragic fires in factories have brought about laws that buildings must be constructed of fireproof materials and be provided with fire escapes. [6]_____ about shocks and burns from electrical [7]_____ have given rise to directives that all such merchandise must be tested before being marketed. Panics and concomitant stampedes in theaters have initiated regulations that exits in places of public gathering must be clearly marked. Sea disasters such as the sinking of the steamship *Titanic* have resulted in orders that ships must carry [8]_____ radios and enough lifeboats to accommodate all the passengers and crew. Explosions and cave-ins have effected provisions that mines and [9]_____ must be shored up and ventilated to remove gas [10]_____.

EXERCISE 202: For each numbered blank in Essay 22, provide the word or phrase which best completes the meaning of the sentence. Make your selection from the numbered groups, which correspond to the numbered blanks. These lists contain words that appeared in Essay 21.

1.	2.	3.	4.
afford	mart	inlets	satin
mow	indifference	precautions	negligence
thrust	range	kindergartens	leak

5.	6.	7.	8.
incompetence	lawns	bubbles	reliable
adequacy	installations	backyards	grumpy
barbecue	complaints	appliances	arrogant

9.	10.
pits	records
sneakers	fumes
canaries	rompers

EXERCISE 203: Pronounce the following words, emphasizing the stressed syllable by saying the vowel louder, longer, and higher in pitch than the other vowels.

A. Emphasize the first syllable of these words:

safety	social	panics	ventilated
hallmark	consciousness	theaters	inlets
present	other	exits	kindergartens
century	factors	places	satin
businesses	movement	public	negligence
realize	tragic	gathering	adequacy
attitude	factories	clearly	barbecue
companies	buildings	sinking	bubbles
order	fireproof	steamship	backyards
workmen's	given	carry	grumpy
over	merchandise	radios	arrogant
mention	tested	lifeboats	sneakers
business	being	passengers	rompers
charges	marketed	cave-ins	

B. Emphasize the second syllable of these words:

endeavor	constructed	disasters	indifference
insure	materials	titanic	precautions
become	provided	resulted	incompetence
efficiency	escapes	enough	complaints
moreover	electrical	accommodate	appliances

insurance	directives	explosions	reliable
concerned	before	effected	canaries
decrease	concomitant	provisions	
competitors	stampedes	remove	
about	initiated	afford	

C. Emphasize the third syllable of these words:

compensation   litigation   regulations   installations

D. Emphasize the fourth syllable of this word:

humanitarianism

EXERCISE 204: Read Essay 22 aloud with the blanks filled in.

EXERCISE 205: Be prepared to answer any questions on Essay 22 that the teacher may ask.

EXERCISE 206: Give an oral summary of Essay 22.

EXERCISE 207: Write a summary of Essay 22.

EXERCISE 208: Write the parts of Essay 22 that the teacher dictates.

EXERCISE 209: Write a composition on a topic suggested by Essay 22.

EXERCISE 210: Answer the following questions, which contain words from Essays 21 and 22.

1. Do automobiles have gas-powered motors?
2. Do you take precautions when you cross a busy street?

3. Does a reckless driver apparently not care very much about safety?
4. Are fumes in a garage dangerous?
5. Can you be accused of negligence if you perform a duty carefully?
6. Is a vacuum cleaner a home appliance?
7. Would you be pleased if you were fired from a job because of incompetence?
8. If you feel indifference about something, are you enthusiastic about it?
9. Do men tell business secrets to their competitors?
10. Where do you take shoes that need repair?
11. Does confidence come from experience?
12. Do you use your dictionary a great deal?
13. What well-known politician was a house painter at one time?
14. Do you wash your own clothes?
15. Does a completely honest person express his thoughts frankly?
16. When a child makes a mistake, do you charge it to his lack of experience?
17. Does a school in this city have any records on you?
18. Do you find a park here and there in this city?
19. Is your English adequate for a conversation with native speakers?
20. What will be the result if you strike a match in a room filled with gas?
21. Do you enjoy a feeling of fatigue?
22. Do most employees want to get an increase in their salary?
23. Have you been in this city for a number of years?
24. What kind of meat is used in a hamburger?
25. Will this season continue for at least another month?
26. Have you bought any paper recently?
27. How many mothers-in-law does a married man usually have?
28. Which clothing store do you usually deal with?
29. Is there a lack of transportation in this city?
30. What kind of news shocks you?
31. Do you get weary of hearing people complain?
32. What color are most of the walls in this building painted?
33. What are good grades based on?
34. Has a friend of yours ever said anything that hurt you?

35. How do you adjust the volume of a radio?
36. Are some fires the work of insane people?
37. Have you ever heard a woman say that her housework never seems finished?
38. Are you working as well as going to school?
39. Do you like the treatment you receive at most stores in this city?
40. Does a work strike sometimes cause great inconvenience?
41. If a student makes bad grades, is he apparently not working hard enough?
42. Do bubbles form in a glass of water after it has stood for a while?
43. Do you board at the place where you stay?
44. In what sort of store can you buy many different kinds of merchandise?
45. Does the house where you live have a lawn?
46. To which department in a large store would you go to buy a suit?
47. Do you care very much about getting an education?
48. Are you looking forward to your next vacation?
49. Would the death of a close friend cause you grief?
50. Have you ever had to be saved from drowning?

EXERCISE 211: Write an essay on one of the questions in Exercise 210.

ESSAY 23 PUSSY WILLOWS

BY ALICE GREEN FREDMAN

When we were children, we lived in Wellesley, a New England
town about 12 miles from Boston. I suppose by today's standards the town would be a suburb, at a convenient, even fashionable, distance from the activities of a busy capital city.
However, it never seemed a suburb to us then. Brookline,
Chestnut Hill—those were suburbs (indeed, they are part of
Greater Boston). Wellesley was something different. True, it
was near enough to Boston for one's father to take the 8:20
to work every morning and the 5:25 home each evening, but
that was part of the adult world and did not concern us. For
us, Wellesley was remote, a little town set away from the
excitement and noise of cities.

Perhaps we felt that way because our trips to the city were
such rare and wondrous occasions. We used to wake up on
those special days twitching with nervousness. We would fidget
and fuss, dreadfully afraid we would miss the train. Once we
got on the train, we would spend the entire ride (it could not
have been very long since it was only 10 or 12 miles) with our
noses pressed tightly against the grimy window panes, peering
anxiously through the black smoke from the coal engine for the
first sign that we were approaching Back Bay Station.

Once we were in the city, we felt that we were in another
world. The dingy buildings, the narrow, crowded streets were
all throbbing with some hidden excitement for us. We were
allowed to go to our father's office and look down (from perhaps no more than five floors) at the train yards and warehouses. It was not, I suspect, a very imposing view, but for us
it was like standing on the top of the world. Our hands would
get clammy, little shivers of apprehension would race up our
spines, and we would feel very daring and brave and slightly
dizzy.

Sometimes we were taken to the Thanksgiving Day parade,
and we would take turns perching on our father's shoulders to
see over the crowds of people. Often it was snowing, and the

crowds and the parade would all merge in indistinct forms as though great curtains of gauze were slowly moving between us. Other times we would go to the department stores during the Christmas season and stare at the window displays, the dazzling lights, and the little armies of mournful Santa Clauses who stood on the street corners, wearily ringing their bells.

When we returned home from one of those visits, we would chatter about it for weeks afterwards, reminding each other of all the details, faithfully retracing our steps and visits. And always, always we would promise each other that when we grew up and had little girls of our own, we would take them to the city at least once a week—or, even better, we would live in the city so that our little girls could continually experience that exquisite joy that was ours only a few times a year.

Of course, Wellesley was all right in its way, we admitted. There were actually many things we liked about it: riding our bikes through piles of crackling fall leaves, making tar balls from the sticky surface of the newly oiled streets in July, sledding down the hills by the golf course. We even agreed that so fascinating a city as Boston could never come up to Wellesley for pussy willows.

Gathering pussy willows was one of our great delights. There was a fine copse of them over behind the aqueduct near the golf course. One had to cross slippery grass hillocks and climb through some brambles to reach them, and the ground was soft and marshy and bumpy. Each spring, about the beginning of March, we would start our watch. Every day after school we would trudge through the wet snowdrifts, slipping and falling on the ice-covered puddles if the weather had turned cold after a thaw, and push our way through the branches to see if the pussy willows were out. Perhaps two or three weeks—and a late spring blizzard—would go by. Then, one day, while the air was still chilly but the wind was somehow warmer and gentler, we would struggle over the marsh, breaking through the thin coating of ice and falling into the chilly swamp water, and discover that the pussy willows were ready. We would shout to each other and, forgetful of thorns, wet shoes, and bruised knees, we would clamber over the hillocks to the copse and triumphantly gather the willow branches. We knew, as we turned homeward, that we would be scolded for our torn jackets and our soaking skirts, but we had found our pussy willows.

Now it all seems very long ago; I have not seen Wellesley or Boston for over twenty years. And I have kept my childhood promise and live in a great city. Nevertheless, each year, when I take my little girl to the park and watch her catch at the young budding twigs and stamp on the fresh, new grass, I wish that she could look forward to coming home from the marsh, tired and scratched, with the first pussy willows of spring.

EXERCISE 212: Pronounce the following words, emphasizing the stressed syllable by saying the vowel louder, longer, and higher in pitch than the other vowels.

A. Emphasize the first syllable of these words:

pussy	busy	morning	tightly
willows	capital	evening	grimy
children	city	little	window
Wellesley	never	cities	peering
England	Brookline	wondrous	anxiously
Boston	chestnut	special	engine
standards	greater	twitching	station
suburb	something	nervousness	dingy
even	different	fidget	buildings
fashionable	father	dreadfully	narrow
distance	every	noses	crowded
throbbing	during	crackling	blizzard
hidden	Christmas	making	chilly
office	season	sticky	somehow
warehouses	dazzling	surface	warmer
standing	armies	newly	gentler
clammy	mournful	sledding	struggle
shivers	Santa	fascinating	breaking

very	Clauses	gathering	coating
daring	corners	over	water
slightly	wearily	aqueduct	ready
dizzy	ringing	slippery	clamber
sometimes	visits	hillocks	homeward
taken	chatter	brambles	scolded
perching	afterwards	marshy	jackets
shoulders	faithfully	bumpy	soaking
people	always	slipping	twenty
often	promise	falling	childhood
snowing	better	covered	budding
curtains	actually	puddles	forward
slowly	only	weather	coming
moving	many	after	
other	riding	branches	

B. Emphasize the second syllable of these words:

about	away	suspect	July
suppose	excitement	imposing	agreed
today	perhaps	parade	delights
Thanksgiving	because	between	behind
convenient	occasions	department	beginning
activities	afraid	returned	discover
however	entire	reminding	forgetful
indeed	against	retracing	triumphantly
enough	approaching	continually	ago
concern	another	experience	
remote	allowed	admitted	

C. Emphasize the third syllable of these words:

apprehension   indistinct

D. Emphasize the fourth syllable of this word:

nevertheless

EXERCISE 213:   Read Essay 23 aloud.

EXERCISE 214: Answer the following questions on the basis of Essay 23.

1. In what town did the author live when she was a child?
2. In which part of the United States was that town?
3. How far was it from Boston?
4. What would it probably be called nowadays?
5. What were the names of some of the suburbs?
6. Was Wellesley different from the suburbs?
7. When did the children's father take the train to go to work?
8. When did he return?
9. Were the children interested in such things as train schedules?
10. What was their opinion of Wellesley?
11. What was the possible explanation for their opinion?
12. How would they wake up on the morning of a trip to Boston?
13. Did they worry about missing the trains?
14. What did they do on the train?
15. Why did they do that?
16. How did the children feel in Boston?
17. Were the buildings clean?
18. Were the streets wide?
19. Were there many people on the streets?
20. Where did the children's father work?
21. Were the children permitted to go to their father's office?
22. How did they feel when they looked out of the window?
23. What kind of parade did they sometimes see?
24. Where did they sit?
25. Did it ever snow during the parade?
26. Could the children see very well then?
27. When did they go to the department stores?
28. What did they look at then?
29. Did they talk about their visits later?
30. Did they remember very much about their visits?
31. What did the children promise to do?
32. Did the children dislike Wellesley?
33. What were some of the things they enjoyed doing there?
34. In what way was Wellesley better than Boston?
35. What was one of the children's favorite pastimes?
36. Where was there a group of pussy willows?
37. Was it difficult to get to the pussy willows?
38. When would the children begin expecting the pussy willows?

39. Was there snow at that time?
40. Might there be ice on the little pools of water?
41. How long might it be before the pussy willows would bloom?
42. Was there at times a snow storm in the meanwhile?
43. Was it still cool when the pussy willows began to bloom?
44. Were the children happy when they discovered the flowers?
45. What did they do with the pussy willows?
46. Was their mother angry with them when they came home?
47. How long has it now been since the author was in Boston or Wellesley?
48. Where does she live now?
49. Does she have any children?
50. Where does she take her daughter?
51. What does her daughter do there?
52. Does the author's little girl have the opportunity to gather pussy willows?
53. Did the author have a brother or a sister?

EXERCISE 215: Give an oral summary of Essay 23.

EXERCISE 216: Write a summary of Essay 23.

EXERCISE 217: Write the parts of Essay 23 that the teacher dictates.

EXERCISE 218: Write a composition on a topic suggested by Essay 23.

EXERCISE 219: Answer the following questions, which contain words from Essay 23.

1. Have you ever seen any pussy willows?
2. Is a shiver from excitement like a shiver from cold?
3. Can the sun dazzle you if you look right at it?
4. Do the stars seem remote to you?
5. After you have lost something, do you sometimes retrace your steps?

6. Does an unhappy child frequently look mournful?
7. When children get excited, do they sometimes race around a room?
8. Do you live in a suburb?
9. Why do some department stores have warehouses?
10. Do the tracks of a railroad seem to merge in the distance?
11. When did you first hear about Santa Claus?
12. Is the coronation of a king sometimes a wondrous occasion?
13. Are the walls of this room dingy?
14. At what distance from your eyes do the forms of words in a book become indistinct?
15. If a person says that a poem is exquisite, does he like it?
16. What do you do when your hands get grimy?
17. What is gauze frequently used for?
18. Do children often twitch when they are excited?
19. Are any of the window panes in this room broken?
20. Does your head sometimes throb when you have a headache?
21. When you are nervous, do your hands get clammy?
22. Do you sometimes peer anxiously at the sky when you are waiting for an airplane to arrive?
23. Do you sit on the end of your spine?
24. Is glue sticky?
25. What happens when you suddenly break through a puddle that is covered with ice?
26. Do young children like to clamber over chairs and sofas?
27. Are the surfaces of most streets in this city covered with asphalt?
28. Do you ever see a copse in this city?
29. What does a driver have to do when his windshield gets a coating of ice?
30. Does a politician feel triumphant when he fails to win an election?
31. What is an aqueduct used for?
32. Why do shepherds have to keep watch over their flocks?
33. Do many people ride bikes to work in this city?
34. Have you ever gone sledding down a hill covered with snow?
35. Who would be more likely to trudge up a long flight of steps— a young man or an old man?
36. Does Canada have many blizzards?

37. Do you like to listen to the crackling of a fire?
38. Is a hillock very high?
39. Can a bramble hurt you?
40. What happens when there is a thaw?

EXERCISE 220:   Write an essay on one of the questions in Exercise 219.

ESSAY 24 MOUNTAIN CLIMBING

Probably no other sport [1]_____ mountain climbing for discomforts and hazards. Nonetheless, mountaineers continue to push their painfully slow way up toward dizzying summits, inching along perpendicular rock faces whose surfaces are [2]_____ with an everlasting [3]_____ of ice, [4]_____ through snowdrifts where there is never a [5]_____, skirting yawning crevasses in glaciers, breathing air so cold that it [6]_____, and braving unexpected [7]_____ that blind and freeze. Although some climbers [8]_____ valuable information for geologists and topographers, most enthusiasts freely [9]_____ that they climb mountains simply because they find the sport fascinating.

Modern mountaineering dates from the ascent of the Wetterhorn in 1854 and of the Matterhorn eleven years later, though successful climbs had been made on Mont Blanc, the Finsteraarhorn, the Jungfrau, the Ortler, and Mont Pelvoux some decades before. Lifting itself over 29,000 feet to be the greatest elevation on the globe, Mount Everest, which had long challenged and defeated numerous intrepid explorers, was finally [10]_____ scaled in 1953 by Sir Edmund Hillary of New Zealand and his Sherpa guide, Tensing.

EXERCISE 221: For each numbered blank in Essay 24, provide the word or phrase which best completes the meaning of the sentence. Make your selection from the numbered groups, which correspond to the numbered blanks. These lists contain words that appeared in Essay 23.

1.	2.	3.	4.
sleds	subtle	coating	budding
comes up to	marshy	bike	soaking
breaks through	slippery	aqueduct	trudging

5.	6.	7.	8.
thaw	crackles	bruise	gather
tar	clambers	copses	scold
gauze	edits	blizzards	scratch

9.	10.
admit	obscurely
struggle	bumpily
stamp	triumphantly

EXERCISE 222: Pronounce the following words, emphasizing the stressed syllable by saying the vowel louder, longer, and higher in pitch than the other vowels.

A. Emphasize the first syllable of these words:

probably	glaciers	lifting	coating
other	breathing	over	aqueduct
mountain	braving	greatest	budding
climbing	climbers	Everest	soaking
hazards	valuable	challenged	trudging
painfully	freely	numerous	crackles
toward	simply	finally	clambers
dizzying	fascinating	Edmund	edits
summits	modern	Hillary	bruises
inching	Wetterhorn	Zealand	copses
faces	Matterhorn	Sherpa	blizzards
surfaces	later	Tensing	gather
never	Jungfrau	subtle	struggle
skirting	Ortler	marshy	bumpily
yawning	decades	slippery	

B. Emphasize the second syllable of these words:

discomforts	topographers	Pelvoux	admit
continue	enthusiasts	before	obscurely
along	because	itself	triumphantly
crevasses	ascent	defeated	
although	eleven	intrepid	
geologists	successful	explorers	

C. Emphasize the third syllable of these words:

nonetheless	perpendicular	information
mountaineers	everlasting	mountaineering
Finsteraarhorn	unexpected	elevation

EXERCISE 223: Read Essay 24 aloud with the blanks filled in.

EXERCISE 224: Be prepared to answer any questions on Essay 24 that the teacher may ask.

EXERCISE 225: Give an oral summary of Essay 24.

EXERCISE 226: Write a summary of Essay 24.

EXERCISE 227: Write the parts of Essay 24 that the teacher dictates.

EXERCISE 228: Write a composition on a topic suggested by Essay 24.

EXERCISE 229: Answer the following questions, which contain words from Essays 23 and 24.

1. Has the weather turned cold recently?
2. Have you ever seen a snowdrift that was 6 feet high?

3. Do you feel embarrassed when you slip and fall on the street?
4. Is the air chilly these mornings?
5. Do children find most stories fascinating?
6. Have you ever tried to walk on ice-covered streets?
7. Have you ever got your clothing torn by thorns?
8. When you go walking in the woods, do you sometimes gather wild flowers?
9. Can you see very far when it is snowing?
10. Do you sometimes feel dizzy when you turn around very quickly?
11. When do streets become slippery?
12. Is tar used on the roof of your house?
13. Do women's dresses cover their knees now?
14. Do most children like hard candy balls?
15. Can you run very quickly over marshy ground?
16. Have you been in this city for less than two weeks?
17. Is smoke from a cigarette usually black?
18. What is on the top of your spine?
19. Why do department stores have window displays?
20. Did the adult world concern you when you were a child?
21. Does an automobile engine use coal?
22. How many shoulders do you have?
23. What do you do when you miss a train?
24. Can you look down at the street from this room?
25. Is a stenographer supposed to write down faithfully what her boss dictates to her?
26. Is this room set away from the noise of the city?
27. Does a train increase its speed when it approaches a station?
28. How many corners does this room have?
29. Are your visits to the theater rare?
30. Does a calm person often fuss?
31. Do you have any children of your own?
32. Have you taken a long ride recently?
33. Do you feel slightly warm right now?
34. Do you have to take a certain train at a certain time?
35. When do you usually wake up?
36. Are the corridors of most new buildings narrow?
37. Does the stage of a theater usually have curtains?
38. What is the capital city of this country?

39. Are the streets of this city crowded around noontime?
40. In what month is Thanksgiving Day?
41. What would you like to say to a person who talks continually?
42. Are you busy with activities all day?
43. How long is the Christmas season?
44. Is it a joy to meet good friends whom you have not seen for a long time?
45. Do children sometimes fidget when they have to sit for a long time?
46. When two persons have a conversation, do they take turns talking?
47. Do you write notes to remind yourself of certain past events?
48. Was yesterday a fine day?
49. How do you feel when you cannot keep a promise?
50. Do you think that Columbus was actually the first European to arrive in America?

EXERCISE 230: Write an essay on one of the questions in Exercise 229.

ESSAY 25 THE CIRCUS

The modern circus and the Roman Circensian games, from which it derives its name, have in common only the aim of entertaining large masses of spectators. The Roman circus was a round or elliptical open-air structure with tiers of seats enclosing a space in which horse and chariot races, athletic exhibitions, and combats between gladiators took place. The American circus is a traveling tent show with rare animals, [1]_____ acrobats whose feats make [2]_____ of apprehension [3]_____ the viewers' spines, clowns who fascinate the children so that they forget to [4]_____ and fuss, and [5]_____ freaks in sideshows. The Roman games were customarily brutal; intimately associated with them is the circus of Nero, where many of the persecuted early Christians perished. The American circus is [6]_____, exciting, but seldom dangerous. With it is associated the master showman P. T. Barnum, who exhibited the famous dwarf General Tom Thumb, managed the highly successful tour of the Swedish singer Jenny Lind, and imported from then [7]_____ Africa the giant elephant Jumbo, whose successors on the morning of the circus's arrival small boys still trail from the [8]_____ to the circus grounds [9]_____ at a [10]_____ distance from the center of town.

EXERCISE 231: For each numbered blank in Essay 25, provide the word or phrase which best completes the meaning of the sentence. Make your selection from the numbered groups, which correspond to the numbered blanks. These lists contain words that appeared in Essays 21 to 24.

1.	2.	3.	4.
daring	shivers	merge	retrace
indistinct	warehouses	race up	fidget
fashionable	curtains	peer	resume

5.	6.	7.	8.
harmonic	weary	remote	panes
wondrous	mournful	grimy	train yards
homeopathic	dazzling	dizzy	throbs

9.	10.
twitched	dingy
set away	convenient
perched on	clammy

EXERCISE 232: Pronounce the following words, emphasizing the stressed syllable by saying the vowel louder, longer, and higher in pitch than the other vowels.

A. Emphasize the first syllable of these words:

circus	acrobats	showman	distance
modern	viewers	Barnum	center
Roman	fascinate	famous	daring
common	children	general	fashionable
only	sideshows	managed	shivers
masses	brutal	highly	warehouses
spectators	intimately	Swedish	curtains
open	Nero	singer	fidget
structure	persecuted	Jenny	wondrous
chariot	early	Africa	mournful
races	Christians	giant	dazzling
combats	perished	elephant	grimy
gladiators	seldom	Jumbo	dizzy
traveling	dangerous	morning	dingy
animals	master	circus's	clammy

B. Emphasize the second syllable of these words:

Circensian	American	imported	remote
derives	forget	successors	away
elliptical	associated	arrival	convenient
enclosing	exciting	retrace	
athletic	exhibited	resume	
between	successful	harmonic	

C. Emphasize the third syllable of these words:

entertaining	apprehension
exhibition	indistinct
customarily	

D. Emphasize the fourth syllable of this word:

homeopathic

EXERCISE 233: Read Essay 25 aloud with the blanks filled in.

EXERCISE 234: Be prepared to answer any questions on Essay 25 that the teacher may ask.

EXERCISE 235: Give an oral summary of Essay 25.

EXERCISE 236: Write a summary of Essay 25.

EXERCISE 237: Write the parts of Essay 25 that the teacher dictates.

EXERCISE 238: Write a composition on a topic suggested by Essay 25.

EXERCISE 239: Answer the following questions, which contain words from Essays 21 to 25.

1. What color is grass?
2. If you have a charge account, do you pay when you make a purchase?
3. Do you dislike to admit a mistake?
4. Does time seem to go by quickly at a party when you are having a good time?
5. When is the ground soft?
6. What things can make you dreadfully afraid?
7. Are you daring if you do something that you know is not dangerous?
8. Do you think of the North Pole as being the top of the world?
9. Does an automatic washing machine require special installation?
10. How many days are there before the beginning of next month?
11. Do people usually shout to each other in a classroom?
12. Does your childhood seem very long ago?
13. Does this building have more than three floors?
14. Would you like to spend your entire time sleeping?
15. When do you walk wearily?
16. Would a person be doing you a favor if he sold you a car that was ten years old?
17. Are most tree branches covered with leaves right now?
18. How many people in this room have on jackets?
19. When people are walking in the Sahara Desert, do they sometimes have to struggle over sandy areas?
20. Are we about 12 miles from Boston?
21. Do you live at a convenient distance from here?
22. Are there any parades in this city?
23. Do mothers around here take their children out to parks?
24. Do you like to dance with a person who stamps on your feet?
25. Is reading one of your delights?
26. What are some of the first signs of spring?
27. Do you suspect that some people do not enjoy the same things that you do?
28. When people chatter about something, is it usually something important?

29. Why is oil put on unpaved streets?
30. Once you agree to something, do you try to fulfill the agreement?
31. Do you bleed when you bruise your hand?
32. Do you sometimes have a feeling of apprehension when the telephone rings late at night?
33. Do groups of children going to school look like little armies?
34. Is this area part of a large city?
35. When do leaves come out on most trees?
36. What kind of flower has thorns?
37. Do many plants grow in a marsh?
38. If you are standing on the ground, can you see over a high wall?
39. Are certain suburbs fashionable, do you think?
40. If you put your hand on your chest, can you feel your heart throb?
41. Do you sleep under a thin blanket when the weather is very cold?
42. Do men wear skirts in this country?
43. Was the sun hidden by clouds all day yesterday?
44. By your standards, is the weather good here?
45. What would happen if you pressed your hands tightly around somebody's throat?
46. How do you feel when somebody stares at you without speaking?
47. When do most workers turn homeward in this city?
48. Are you looking forward to having a vacation soon?
49. Where do birds usually perch?
50. Have you got on a train recently?
51. Do cows wear bells, do you know?
52. Does a person express complete approval when he says that something is all right in its way?
53. Have you ever watched a kitten catching at its tail?
54. In what month does fall begin in this country?
55. Does an architect have to put a lot of details in a design for a building?
56. What is inspected at train yards?
57. Do you like to experience an unpleasant feeling?
58. What happens when you ride over a bumpy road?

59. What kinds of animals live in swamps?
60. Is July warmer than December in this city?
61. In what country did you grow up?
62. What are some days that are special for you?
63. Do you sometimes have to push your way through a crowd?
64. Do you enjoy being scolded for something you have done?
65. When can you find budding twigs?
66. Do your teachers have piles of papers to correct?
67. What is a golf course used for?
68. Do you ever get so interested in a book that you become forgetful of the time?
69. Do you feel comfortable in soaking clothes?
70. What kind of domestic animal can scratch you?
71. Has this day come up to your expectations?
72. Do most trees lose their leaves before winter?
73. How long does it take you to reach this room from your home?
74. When do you find puddles in the street?
75. Is the climate in Ethiopia gentler than in England?
76. Why should you take off wet shoes?

EXERCISE 240: Write an essay on one of the questions in Exercise 239.

UNIT **6**

ESSAY 26 MEMORIES OF DYLAN THOMAS AS A READER

BY KARL BECKSON

When the Welsh poet Dylan Thomas died in New York in 1953, the world lost not only a great poet but also a great reader. His resonant voice, emerging with terrifying force from his short body, had brought lyric and dramatic poetry wonderfully alive. He had given his audiences a new emotional awareness of the magic, the power, the inner vibration of language.

I first saw and heard Thomas during his initial visit to the United States in 1950. He drew enormous numbers of curious people who had been acquainted only with his published verse and who wished to see the brilliant young poet. On that night he was introduced by another poet, John Malcolm Brinnin, who described Thomas as perhaps the most promising poet of our century.

Following the introduction, Thomas came out on the stage with uncertainty. His appearance was disappointing: His fleshy, round face, his curly reddish-brown hair, his surprisingly short body, and his unpressed suit of heavy tweeds gave an impression of a shabby, earthbound cherub. Acknowledging the audience's applause with a nod, he announced in a low voice that he would begin with several poems of a fellow Welsh poet, W. H. Davies. As he spoke, I could see that his teeth were in a ruined state: Some were discolored, some missing. He then began to read.

His voice was rich in tone, without the affectations of the usual reader of verse. Each poem was given with the sustained power of an oration, with an intensity of feeling that politicians might admire. The printed word came alive with a new dimension of meaning.

He concluded his program with a reading of the last scene of Christopher Marlowe's *Dr. Faustus*. The terror of damnation, the desperate wish for salvation in Faustus's great line, "See, see where Christ's blood streams in the firmament!"

surged through Thomas's voice with supreme elevation of spirit.

I next saw Thomas when he gave a special reading at Columbia University. When he appeared on the platform, he was obviously drunk. He stopped in front of the lectern, looked down at a tall, slender pitcher of water which had been set out for him, and said in a slurred voice, "That's the biggest glass of water I've ever seen!" Only a few people laughed. Many wondered whether he would be able to read effectively. After a somewhat unsteady beginning, he soon recaptured the force and control of his voice. His reading of the poetry was inspired.

Thomas's drunkenness continued. Rumors circulated that he could not face an audience without the support of alcohol. If it was true, Thomas had an amazing capacity for self-control, for people rarely suspected that he had taken several drinks before a reading.

Before he died in an alcoholic coma in a New York hospital, Thomas made a number of recordings of his poetry and one recording of his play *Under Milk Wood*, in which he is the narrator. They capture the lyrical intensity of that voice which is now still.

EXERCISE 241: Pronounce the following words, emphasizing the stressed syllable by saying the vowel louder, longer, and higher in pitch than the other vowels.

A. Emphasize the first syllable of these words:

memories	people	reader	ever
Dylan	only	given	many
Thomas	published	feeling	wondered
reader	brilliant	printed	whether
poet	Malcolm	meaning	able
also	Brinnin	program	after
resonant	promising	reading	somewhat
terrifying	century	Christopher	drunkenness

body	curious	missing	pitcher
lyric	following	usual	water
poetry	fleshy	Marlowe	biggest
wonderfully	curly	Faustus	rumors
given	reddish	terror	circulated
audiences	heavy	desperate	alcohol
magic	shabby	firmament	coma
power	earthbound	spirit	hospital
inner	cherub	special	number
language	several	platform	under
during	poem	obviously	narrator
visit	fellow	lectern	capture
numbers	Davies	slender	lyrical

B. Emphasize the second syllable of these words:

emerging	perhaps	without	effectively
dramatic	uncertainty	sustained	unsteady
alive	appearance	oration	beginning
emotional	surprisingly	intensity	recaptured
awareness	unpressed	admire	control
vibration	impression	dimension	inspired
initial	acknowledging	concluded	continued
United	applause	damnation	support
enormous	announced	salvation	amazing
acquainted	begin	supreme	capacity
another	discolored	Columbia	recording
described	began	appeared	

C. Emphasize the third syllable of these words:

introduced	disappointing	politicians	university
introduction	affectations	elevation	

EXERCISE 242: Read Essay 26 aloud.

EXERCISE 243: Answer the following questions on the basis of Essay 26.

1. What country was Thomas a native of?
2. Where and when did he die?
3. What were two accomplishments that he had?
4. Did he have an attractive voice?
5. What was his height?
6. Could Thomas read poetry aloud effectively?
7. When did he first go to the United States?
8. What was the purpose of his trip?
9. Did many people go to hear him?
10. Had he published any poetry by then?
11. What was the vocation of the man who introduced Thomas to the audience?
12. What kind of opinion did that man have of Thomas?
13. What was the initial impression that Thomas gave on the stage?
14. Was he handsome?
15. Was he thin?
16. Was Thomas bald?
17. What did the author of the essay compare Thomas with?
18. How did Thomas react to the audience's applause?
19. Did he begin by reading his own poetry?
20. Why do you think the author noticed Thomas's teeth?
21. What was the condition of Thomas's teeth?
22. Did Thomas sound like the usual professional reader?
23. Did he give the impression of being interested in what he was reading?
24. Did he seem to understand what he was reading?
25. What was the last thing that he read?
26. What feeling was conveyed when Thomas read the line that the author mentions?
27. Where did the author see Thomas again?
28. What was Thomas's condition at that time?
29. What did he make an unexpected comment about?
30. What was the reaction of the audience?
31. How did Thomas sound when he began his reading?
32. Was his whole performance a failure?
33. Did Thomas give up drinking?
34. What did some people say was the reason for his addiction?

35. Was his drunkenness often apparent?
36. In what condition was Thomas when he died?
37. What had he recorded?
38. Were the recordings very effective?

EXERCISE 244: Give an oral summary of Essay 26.

EXERCISE 245: Write a summary of Essay 26.

EXERCISE 246: Write the parts of Essay 26 that the teacher dictates.

EXERCISE 247: Write a composition on a topic suggested by Essay 26.

EXERCISE 248: Answer the following questions, which contain words from Essay 26.

1. Do you have memories about any great performer?
2. How do you feel when you have an elevation of spirit—good or bad?
3. Is a brilliant young pianist sometimes called a prodigy?
4. What kind of person makes it his business to keep people's teeth from getting into a ruined state?
5. In which country is Welsh spoken?
6. Is the consumption of alcohol condemned by any religion you know?
7. Is a psychiatrist interested in the inner life of his patients?
8. What does a speaker put on a lectern?
9. Which would more likely be described as earthbound—an artist or businessman?
10. When a man is drowning, do you suppose he has a desperate wish for salvation?
11. Are most boys and girls slender when they are about fifteen?
12. When you are delirious, do you have any control over your thoughts?
13. Does a coma last a long time?
14. How does a stage performer usually acknowledge applause?

15. Does a pitcher of iced tea look inviting in hot weather?
16. What are some of the things that are in the firmament?
17. When is terror more likely to surge through a person's voice—when he is afraid or when he is happy?
18. When we say that a word or sentence is beautiful, are we having an emotional reaction?
19. Who is the narrator of an autobiography?
20. Do you find it difficult to understand a poem when a person reads it effectively?
21. Is Shakespeare's voice now still?
22. In what kind of room would you find a platform?
23. Does a portrait painter try to capture the personality of his subject?
24. After you have been sick, do you feel unsteady when you first get out of bed?
25. Why is a speaker usually introduced to the audience by someone else?
26. Do many people you know wear tweeds?
27. Would an atheist worry about damnation?
28. Which is more likely to have a resonant voice—a man or a woman?
29. Is it customary for a well-to-do person to look shabby?
30. Which would more likely be referred to as promising—a young man or an old one?
31. If you were planning to buy a piano, would you want one that was rich in tone?
32. Would it be possible to think of a feeling of sympathy as an emotional vibration?
33. Do you become annoyed with a person who has affectations?
34. What recent discoveries have terrifying force?
35. Does a confident person usually have an air of uncertainty?
36. Does a dwarf have a short or a tall body?
37. On the street does an acquaintance sometimes indicate that he has seen you by giving a nod?
38. Have you seen many people with reddish-brown hair?
39. Do you feel stage fright when you face an audience?
40. Is it easy to be a good public reader?

EXERCISE 249: Write an essay on one of the questions in Exercise 248.

ESSAY 27 PETROLEUM

Man has been [1]_____ with petroleum or "rock oil" throughout historic time; it was described by Herodotus and other ancient writers. Its [2]_____ use was in mortar, for coating walls and boat hulls, and as a fire weapon in defensive warfare, but it was [3]_____ burned for illumination. North American Indians used it in [4]_____, medicine, and paints. In Europe it was scooped from tops of streams or dipped from puddles which formed as it [5]_____ from the ground, and in the early nineteenth century small quantities were extracted from shale. In 1815 several streets in Prague were lighted with petroleum lamps.

The modern petroleum industry began in 1859, when E. L. Drake drilled a producing well in Pennsylvania. An [6]_____ number of wells have been drilled all over the world since then. At first, kerosene was the chief finished product, and kerosene lamps soon [7]_____ the market from whale-oil lamps and candles. With the development of the gasoline engine and its application to automobiles, trucks, tractors, and airplanes, there has been an [8]_____ increase in the use of petroleum. Modern civilization could hardly exist without its [9]_____ for motive [10]_____, lubrication, fuel, dyes, drugs, and synthetics.

EXERCISE 250: For each numbered blank in Essay 27, provide the word or phrase which best completes the meaning of the sentence. Make your selection from the numbered groups, which correspond to the numbered blanks. These lists contain words that appeared in Exercise 26.

1.	2.	3	4.
acquainted	resonant	frigidly	nod
introduced	initial	rarely	lyric
surged	fleshy	shabbily	magic

5.	6.	7.	8.
concluded	earthbound	captured	almanac
suspected	curly	set out	unpressed
emerged	enormous	stitched	amazing

9.	10
support	tweeds
vibration	power
uncertainty	cherub

EXERCISE 251: Pronounce the following words, emphasizing the stressed syllable by saying the vowel louder, longer, and higher in pitch than the other vowels.

A. Emphasize the first syllable of these words:

other	century	candles	frigidly
ancient	quantities	gasoline	rarely
writers	several	engine	shabbily
mortar	lighted	automobiles	lyric
coating	modern	tractors	magic
weapon	industry	airplanes	earthbound
warfare	number	increase	curly
Indians	over	hardly	captured
medicine	kerosene	motive	almanac
Europe	finished	fuel	power
puddles	product	resonant	cherub
early	market	fleshy	

B. Emphasize the second syllable of these words:

petroleum	extracted	acquainted	amazing
throughout	began	initial	support
historic	producing	concluded	vibration
described	development	suspected	uncertainty
Herodotus	exist	emerged	
defensive	without	enormous	
American	synthetics	unpressed	

C. Emphasize the third syllable of these words:

Pennsylvania   application   lubrication   introduced

D. Emphasize the fourth syllable of these words:

illumination   civilization

EXERCISE 252: Read Essay 27 aloud with the blanks filled in.

EXERCISE 253: Be prepared to answer any questions on Essay 27 that the teacher may ask.

EXERCISE 254: Give an oral summary of Essay 27.

EXERCISE 255: Write a summary of Essay 27.

EXERCISE 256: Write the parts of Essay 27 that the teacher dictates.

EXERCISE 257: Write a composition on a topic suggested by Essay 27.

EXERCISE 258: Answer the following questions, which contain words from Essays 26 and 27.

1. Through what openings can your voice emerge?
2. Does a host customarily feel obligated to sustain a conversation with a guest?
3. Do you need the support of anesthesia when a dentist fills one of your teeth?
4. Would it be an exaggeration to say that a poem exerts a kind of magic when it has a strong effect on our emotions?
5. Does an obviously nervous person have an amazing capacity for self-control?

6. What ancient writers do you know?
7. Would it be reasonable for a politician to address voters as "fellow citizens"?
8. Do you use kerosene in your home?
9. As a child develops emotional reactions toward his surroundings, does his environment take on new dimensions of meaning for him?
10. What is the largest industry in this country?
11. Can a poem be read in a way so that you gain a new awareness of its beauty?
12. Does a farmer hope to have a market for his products?
13. Did it take you a surprisingly short time to learn English?
14. Which fuel is most widely used for motive power?
15. With what is the usual dinner concluded?
16. Is the weather somewhat warm today?
17. What do you say when you are introduced to someone?
18. Would you expect to see a businessman in his office in an unpressed suit?
19. Are your teeth likely to get discolored if you do not brush them regularly?
20. Do young children usually enjoy watching love scenes in a play?
21. What weapons are used in warfare nowadays?
22. What notable person has the world lost recently?
23. Would a child be likely to ask his mother for a favor when she was obviously angry?
24. Does music sometimes have the power to calm you when you are feeling upset?
25. If an adult has thirty teeth, are some missing?
26. Which kind of news is said to circulate faster—good news or bad?
27. Do you prefer to see movies from the beginning?
28. Why is it not a good idea to read tales of terror right before you go to bed?
29. After a person is fifty, is he likely to recapture the vitality he had when he was eighteen?
30. When you read a novel, do you enjoy wondering how the story will end?
31. What could give you supreme joy?

32. Have tears ever streamed down your face when you were very cold?

33. Which kind of actor do you prefer—one who gives an inspired reading of his lines or one who says them mechanically?

34. Does a chairman often begin a meeting with reports from committees?

35. Does an accident draw crowds of curious people?

36. Is your hair curly?

37. Who sets out instruments for a surgeon before an operation?

38. Have you ever heard a recording of your own voice?

39. Is it the intention of an actor to bring a playwright's words alive?

40. Do you believe all the rumors you hear?

41. What is mortar used for?

42. What are the chief means of illumination these days?

43. How many wheels do most trucks have?

44. How long can you exist without water?

45. Are you wearing any synthetics at the moment?

46. Where would you go to buy drugs?

47. Is the hull of something its outside or its inside?

48. Can you scoop fish from puddles around here?

49. When a dentist pulls one of your teeth, does he drill it or extract it?

50. How long is historic time?

EXERCISE 259: Write an essay on one of the questions in Exercise 258.

ESSAY 28 JAZZ

BY LOUIS H. LEVI

What is jazz? An anecdote, doubtless apocryphal, describes
a bewildered matron asking that question of Louis Armstrong,
to which Armstrong is said to have replied that if she had to
ask what it was, she did not have it. Jazz does elude definition.
However, the key, the "it" that the uninitiated do not have,
is probably an ability to sense the beat, the driving force, sometimes powerful, sometimes subtle, that must be felt by musicians and audience alike if the one is to create and the other
to appreciate jazz.

So crucial is the maintenance of the rhythmic underpinning
that it constitutes very nearly a full-time job for four (piano,
string bass, guitar, and drums) of the seven instruments (add
trumpet, clarinet, and trombone) that make up the standard
traditional jazz combination. Nevertheless, the insistent four-
beats-to-the-bar march rhythm does not alone make jazz the
exciting thing it is. As a matter of fact, a trumpet player winging away on a solo flight is scarcely aware that that foundation
exists although he subconsciously appreciates its support. He
has his mind on his own creation of an infinitely complex
pattern of counter-rhythms, syncopations, and accents falling
ahead of and behind the beat, a tantalizing and at times baffling variety of rhythmic surprises. "The effect," says jazz
historian Marshall Stearns, "is schizophrenic, like rubbing your
stomach in one direction and the top of your head in another."
The continual tension between two sets of rhythms, the underlying beat and the superimposed variations of the improvising
instrumentalists, gives jazz much of its unique quality.

Once a tune falls into the hands of a jazz musician, it stands
to lose much of its identity. Just as the foundation rhythm
serves as a point of departure for the jazzman's polyrhythmic
complications, so does the written melody, a kind of persistent
whisper in the back of his head, provide a takeoff point for his
melodic excursions. Performer becomes composer, elaborating
certain phrases and eliminating others, interpolating his own

musical ideas, and ultimately bringing forth an unmistakably individual re-creation of the original composition.

Melodically, however, the jazzman's liberty is restrained, to an extent that his rhythmic inventiveness is not, by the necessity of basing his improvisations on the harmonies, the sequence of chords appropriate to the basic melody. That harmonic structure is, in fact, the cement of the jazz group, the discipline that keeps the wandering impulses of its members within reasonable bounds. Without such discipline, collective improvisation would be out of the question; with it, each musician is able to anticipate roughly what the others will do, and this, along with the fact that each instrument tends to take a traditional role in the ensemble, makes it possible for musicians to sit down together for the first time and produce jazz without the benefit of a single sheet of musical manuscript.

If the jazzman's rhythmic and melodic improvisations are the basic ingredients of the music he produces, the spice of the mixture is its spontaneity. No jazz performance exactly duplicates any other. To be sure, the order in which the soloists take their choruses may be prearranged, some of the ensemble figures may be planned in advance, and in the larger jazz organizations there is necessarily a good deal of rehearsed section work. Nonetheless, within this framework the jazzman remains free to follow whatever paths are pointed out to him by the interaction of his own inspiration with that of his fellow musicians.

The essence of jazz and the reasons for its magnetism remain elusive. Perhaps the answer lies in the flexibility of the performance and its capacity for producing the unexpected. Perhaps it is the combined appeal of the primitive and the sophisticated, the intense rhythms of the West African jungle coupled with a profuseness of melodic invention that is the envy of classical composers. Or perhaps the explanation is as simple as that offered to a Library of Congress musicologist by the late Jelly Roll Morton, one of the greatest of the New Orleans blues and ragtime pianists. "Jazz music," he said, "is to be played sweetly, softly, with plenty of rhythm. When you have your rhythm with your swing, it becomes beautiful."

EXERCISE 260: Pronounce the following words, emphasizing the stressed syllable by saying the vowel louder, longer, and higher in pitch than the other vowels.

A. Emphasize the first syllable of these words:

anecdote	matter	musical	section
doubtless	player	ultimately	framework
matron	winging	bringing	follow
asking	solo	liberty	pointed
question	scarcely	basing	fellow
Louis	infinitely	harmonies	essence
Armstrong	pattern	sequence	reasons
probably	counter	basic	magnetism
driving	accents	structure	answer
sometimes	falling	discipline	primitive
powerful	tantalizing	wandering	African
subtle	baffling	impulses	jungle
audience	Marshall	members	coupled
other	rubbing	reasonable	envy
crucial	stomach	question	classical
maintenance	continual	roughly	simple
rhythmic	tension	possible	offered
underpinning	underlying	benefit	library
constitutes	improvising	manuscript	congress
very	quality	mixture	jelly
nearly	into	duplicates	Morton
seven	jazzman	any	greatest
instrument	written	order	ragtime
trumpet	melody	soloists	sweetly
trombone	whisper	choruses	softly
standard	certain	figures	plenty
rhythm	phrases	larger	beautiful

B. Emphasize the second syllable of these words:

apocryphal	although	performer	together
describes	subconsciously	becomes	produce
bewildered	support	composer	ingredients
replied	creation	elaborating	performance
elude	complex	eliminating	exactly
however	ahead	interpolating	advance
ability	behind	ideas	rehearsed
musician	variety	original	remains
alike	surprises	melodically	whatever
create	effect	restrained	elusive
appreciate	historian	extent	perhaps
piano	direction	inventiveness	capacity
guitar	another	necessity	combined
traditional	between	appropriate	appeal
insistent	unique	harmonic	sophisticated
alone	identity	within	intense
exciting	departure	without	profuseness
away	persistent	collective	invention
aware	provide	anticipate	pianists
foundation	melodic	along	
exists	excursions	ensemble	

C. Emphasize the third syllable of these words:

definition	schizophrenic	individual	inspiration
uninitiated	variations	composition	flexibility
necessarily	instrumentalists	spontaneity	unexpected
clarinet	polyrhythmic	prearranged	re-creation
combination	complications	nonetheless	musicologist
syncopation	unmistakably	interaction	

D. Emphasize the fourth syllable of these words:

nevertheless	superimposed	improvisation	organizations

EXERCISE 261: Read Essay 28 aloud.

1. Is the story about the musician Louis Armstrong and the woman unquestionably true?
2. What did the woman ask Armstrong?
3. How did she feel when she asked the question?
4. What was his answer?
5. Is it easy to define jazz?
6. What is probably the most important element in jazz?
7. Do all inexperienced people feel the rhythm?
8. Is the beat always strong?
9. Does the beat have to be sensed only by the players?
10. Which instruments are primarily used to maintain the rhythm?
11. Which other instruments are there in the usual jazz group?
12. How many regular stresses are there to a measure?
13. Is the rhythmic pattern similar to that usually played by a military band?
14. Does a horn player sometimes play a tune that superficially seems unrelated to the basic rhythm?
15. Is his tune actually closely related to the basic pattern?
16. Did one man compare jazz to a kind of mental disorder?
17. Is the varying of the basic rhythm by the solo instruments greatly responsible for the distinctiveness of jazz?
18. Is a jazz musician likely to change a tune?
19. What does he change besides the rhythm?
20. Does he expand certain phrases?
21. Does he omit other phrases?
22. Does he insert original ideas?
23. Is the jazz musician's rendition of the composition very individualistic?
24. What must the musician observe in a composition?
25. Do the harmonies restrict him to a certain extent?
26. Do the other musicians have a fair idea of what an improviser is going to do?
27. Can jazz musicians play together without rehearsal?
28. Can musicians play together without written scores?
29. Is the lack of premeditation an enjoyable part of jazz?
30. Is each performance a novelty?
31. Are parts of a performance sometimes arranged in advance?

32. What is the major guide to a jazz musician?
33. What are some possible explanations for the attraction of jazz?

EXERCISE 263: Give an oral summary of Essay 28.

EXERCISE 264: Write a summary of Essay 28.

EXERCISE 265: Write the parts of Essay 28 that the teacher dictates.

EXERCISE 266: Write a composition on a topic suggested by Essay 28.

EXERCISE 267: Answer the following questions, which contain words from Essay 28.

1. Do musicians play jazz in this country?
2. Is a string bass a large or small instrument?
3. Is a guitar very heavy?
4. How many measures of music are contained between two bars?
5. Does a reliable newspaper usually print apocryphal reports?
6. Who are some composers who created great music?
7. Can you make a noise like thunder on a drum?
8. What is superimposed on the front of a book?
9. Is a trumpet a horn or a string instrument?
10. Do witnesses sometimes give quite different versions of an incident?
11. Are some animals supposed to have the ability to sense danger?
12. Do surprises make life an exciting thing for children?
13. Do you suspect that teachers are quite used to hearing students improvise excuses for not being prepared?
14. Do piano students sometimes use a metronome as an aid to get the correct beat of a musical composition?
15. Do you sometimes get the impression that a singer is winging away like a bird, forgetful of his audience?
16. Is an orchestra composed entirely of instrumentalists?

17. What is the underpinning of a dock usually made of?
18. Does syncopation serve to vary the rhythm of a musical composition?
19. Is anger a powerful emotion?
20. Which would probably cost more—a standard model or a custom-built car?
21. When you walk, does your right foot go in one direction and your left in another?
22. Once you have seen a movie, do you usually like to see it again?
23. Do you imagine that seamen get wandering impulses after staying on land for a while?
24. What do you think of Thomas A. Edison's remark "Genius is one per cent inspiration and ninety-nine per cent perspiration"?
25. Would you like to fall into the hands of an executioner?
26. How many members are there right now in the United Nations?
27. Is a musical figure long or short?
28. Is a guest supposed to offer an explanation when he is late?
29. When a person uses certain words, is he unmistakably angry?
30. Does the expression "to be sure" often mean the same as "of course"?
31. Name some of the countries of West Africa.
32. When a lecturer talks about something that is not immediately related to his stated topic, is he taking an excursion?
33. What do you think is a reasonable price for a textbook?
34. Would you say that a charming person had a kind of magnetism?
35. Do you suspect that a criminal would like to change his identity?
36. Do movies often portray a re-creation of a historic event?
37. What are the basic ingredients of bread?
38. Does a scientist need curiosity coupled with persistence?
39. What is the customary term for a performer on a piano?
40. When a person says that a request is out of the question, does he mean that he will grant it?

EXERCISE 268: Write an essay on one of the questions in Exercise 267.

ESSAY 29 PSYCHIATRY

Psychiatry is the division of medicine which deals with the diagnosis and treatment of mental diseases or, to use the [1]_____ term of those [2]_____ in the science, insanity. The [3]_____ causes of mental disturbance may be either organic—that is, due to physical damage to or impairment of the nervous system—or functional, for which there is no observable evidence of physical disability or malfunctioning. According to psychiatrists like Freud, [4]_____ conflicts in the personality lay the [5]_____ for the functional disorders.

Mental illnesses are also differentiated, primarily on a quantitative basis, into neuroses and psychoses. A neurosis, somewhat less serious than a psychosis, may exhibit itself in persistent fatigue, constant [6]_____, feelings of anxiety, [7]_____ unwanted thoughts, compulsive acts, or bodily ailments. On the other hand, a psychosis renders its victim incapable of adjusting realistically to his environment. The symptoms may include, either separately or in [8]_____, hallucinations and delusions, intense depression or mania, lack or inappropriateness of outward emotional response, and severe distortion of judgment. Among the [9]_____ of organic psychoses are general paresis, senile dementia, and epilepsy. The psychoses which [10]_____ the functional category are schizophrenia (earlier called dementia praecox), paranoia, and manic-depressive psychosis.

EXERCISE 269: For each numbered blank in Essay 29, provide the word or phrase which best completes the meaning of the sentence. Make your selection from the numbered groups, which correspond to the numbered blanks. These lists contain words that appeared in Essay 28.

1.	2.	3.	4.
crucial	sobbing	eluding	smocked
bewildered	uninitiated	underlying	subconscious
traditional	apocryphal	bass	arterial

5.	6.	7.	8.
anecdote	tension	insistent	matron
clarinet	beat	aware	bar
foundation	underpinning	stucco	combination

9.	10.
varieties	make up
trombones	wing away
apaches	superimpose

EXERCISE 270: Pronounce the following words, emphasizing the stressed syllable by saying the vowel louder, longer, and higher in pitch than the other vowels.

A. Emphasize the first syllable of these words:

medicine	conflicts	renders	manic
treatment	illnesses	victim	crucial
mental	also	symptoms	sobbing
science	quantitative	separately	underlying
causes	basis	mania	anecdote
either	somewhat	outward	tension
physical	serious	judgment	underpinning
damage	constant	general	stucco
nervous	feelings	senile	matron
system	bodily	epilepsy	trombones
functional	ailments	category	
evidence	other	praecox	

B. Emphasize the second syllable of these words:

psychiatry	neuroses	environment	depressive
division	psychoses	include	bewildered
diseases	neurosis	delusions	traditional
insanity	psychosis	intense	apocryphal
disturbance	exhibit	depression	eluding
organic	itself	emotional	subconscious
impairment	persistent	response	arterial
observable	fatigue	severe	foundation
malfunctioning	anxiety	distortion	insistent
according	unwanted	among	aware
psychiatrists	compulsive	organic	varieties
disorders	incapable	paresis	apaches
primarily	adjusting	dementia	away

C. Emphasize the third syllable of these words:

diagnosis	differentiated	schizophrenia	clarinet
disability	realistically	paranoia	combination
personality	inappropriateness	uninitiated	

D. Emphasize the fourth syllable of these words:

hallucinations   superimpose

EXERCISE 271: Read Essay 29 aloud with the blanks filled in.

EXERCISE 272: Be prepared to answer any questions on Essay 29 that the teacher may ask.

EXERCISE 273: Give an oral summary of Essay 29.

EXERCISE 274: Write a summary of Essay 29.

EXERCISE 275: Write the parts of Essay 29 that the teacher dictates.

EXERCISE 276: Write a composition on a topic suggested by Essay 29.

EXERCISE 277: Answer the following questions, which contain words from Essays 28 and 29.

1. How many hours a week constitute a full-time job?
2. When a doctor makes a diagnosis, does he rely on the foundation he received in college?
3. Might a guilty man hear a whisper in the back of his head telling him that he had done wrong?
4. Do composers often elaborate simple songs and turn them into complicated musical compositions?
5. Does a leaking water faucet make a persistent noise?
6. Would a very self-restrained person be likely to show surprise at the unexpected?
7. Does there seem to be continual tension between certain countries?
8. Does a fire alarm have an insistent sound?
9. Is a psychiatrist interested in the underlying causes of people's unhappiness?
10. Do you find a variety of merchandise in a drugstore?
11. Might the members of a society refer to nonmembers as "the uninitiated"?
12. Do you think the schedule of flights at a large airport probably has an infinitely complex pattern?
13. Have you ever seen a wall clock that had counterweights hanging down?
14. Does a teacher usually try to reply to any question that a student asks?
15. Is leaving your home similar to a bird's making a solo flight?
16. Do you imagine that a true artist feels a driving force that impels him to work?
17. Do most English words have the accent on the last syllable?
18. Which does a court judge base his decisions on—precedents or his emotional reactions?

19. Are the inhabitants of a small, isolated village likely to be sophisticated?

20. Do you trust that ultimately the work of the United Nations will bring forth solutions to all international problems?

21. Are the sun's rays ordinarily intense in January?

22. What do parents generally provide for their children?

23. Do you like to plan a vacation in advance?

24. Does a merchant stand to lose money if his customers do not pay their bills?

25. How many pages of a book can be put on one sheet of paper?

26. Is the music that is played in a church usually soft or loud?

27. Does a union perform the function of collective bargaining with its members' employer?

28. Would a person be likely to hear ragtime music in a bank?

29. Is legal punishment supposed to be appropriate to the offense?

30. Does the realization of a person's ambition usually lie in his own capacity?

31. Can being from the same city serve as a point of departure for a conversation between strangers?

32. Is growing up a mixture of pleasure and pain?

33. Is a playwright expected to have a good deal of dramatic invention?

34. Is a song made up of phrases?

35. Should a student learn the spelling of a word along with its pronunciation?

36. What modern convenience would probably be the envy of eighteenth-century people who got tired of walking up stairs?

37. Can you name a person who was known for his inventiveness?

38. Do noisy games have an appeal for children?

39. Who are some well-known composers for the piano?

40. Does June 30 fall ahead of July 1?

41. What kind of professional entertainer tells anecdotes?

42. Have you at times been subconsciously aware that you had made a mistake although you did not know exactly what it was?

43. If it rains today, will the streets doubtless get wet?

44. Who tells you that he would appreciate your support in an election?

45. What kind of band frequently plays marches?

46. Does a monotonous tune have too much rhythm or too little rhythm?
47. Was your mother a matron when you were born?
48. Is rubbing the stomach a sign of hunger?
49. Is a historian concerned with fact or fiction?
50. Would you be worried if a psychiatrist told you you were schizophrenic?

EXERCISE 278: Write an essay on one of the questions in Exercise 277.

ESSAY 30 THOMAS A. EDISON

Thomas Alva Edison, who before his death in 1931 had taken out over thirteen hundred United States and foreign patents, is without question the American most noted for his [1]_____. His biography could easily serve as [2]_____ for one of Horatio Alger's dime novels with the title of *From Rags to Riches or Never Say Die*. A self-taught genius (his formal schooling was limited to three months in 1854), Edison became a newsboy at the age of twelve and a telegraph operator soon afterwards. The most outstanding of his inventions had to do with electricity and reproduction of sound. His wax-cylinder phonograph, patented in 1878 when he was thirty-one, was the first successful [3]_____ for the [4]_____ of sound, though the modern disk is [5]_____ derived from a basic improvement by Emile Berliner. Following the [6]_____ that had been pointed out by fellow inventors, Edison [7]_____ the first commercially practical incandescent electric lamp in 1879 and two years later constructed the world's first central electric-light power plant in New York City. He developed the kinetoscope or "peep show" machine, one of the numerous forerunners of the modern motion picture, and later demonstrated experimentally the synchronization of moving pictures and sound; talking pictures were [8]_____ on his work. Not known for [9]_____ into the realm of abstract science, Edison was [10]_____ a prodigy in the practical application of scientific principles.

EXERCISE 279: For each numbered blank in Essay 30, provide the word or phrase which best completes the meaning of the sentence. Make your selection from the numbered groups, which correspond to the numbered blanks. These lists contain words that appeared in Essays 26 to 29.

1.	2.	3.	4.
sequence	tune	identity	role
inventiveness	inspiration	instrument	ingredient
soloist	harmony	chord	re-creation

5.	6.	7.	8.
ultimately	paths	restrained	based
laconically	spice	sniffled	interpolated
profusely	spontaneity	brought forth	cemented

9.	10.
melody	elusively
excursions	collectively
whisper	unmistakably

EXERCISE 280: Pronounce the following words, emphasizing the stressed syllable by saying the vowel louder, longer, and higher in pitch than the other vowels.

A. Emphasize the first syllable of these words:

Thomas	never	Berliner	talking
Alva	genius	following	science
Edison	formal	pointed	prodigy
taken	schooling	fellow	practical
over	limited	practical	principles
hundred	newsboy	later	sequence
foreign	telegraph	central	soloist
patents	operator	power	harmony
question	afterwards	city	instrument
noted	cylinder	numerous	ultimately
easily	phonograph	forerunner	sniffled
Alger	patented	motion	melody
novels	thirty	picture	whisper
title	modern	demonstrated	
riches	basic	moving	

B. Emphasize the second syllable of these words:

before	successful	developed	restrained
united	derived	kinetoscope	interpolated
without	improvement	machine	cemented
American	Emile	inventiveness	excursions
biography	inventors	identity	elusively
Horatio	commercially	ingredient	collectively
became	electric	laconically	
inventions	constructed	profusely	

C. Emphasize the third syllable of these words:

electricity	application	re-creation
reproduction	scientific	spontaneity
incandescent	inspiration	unmistakably

D. Emphasize the fourth syllable of these words:

experimentally   synchronization

EXERCISE 281:   Read Essay 30 aloud with the blanks filled in.

EXERCISE 282:   Be prepared to answer any questions on Essay 30 that the teacher may ask.

EXERCISE 283:   Give an oral summary of Essay 30.

EXERCISE 284:   Write a summary of Essay 30.

EXERCISE 285:   Write the parts of Essay 30 that the teacher dictates.

EXERCISE 286:   Write a composition on a topic suggested by Essay 30.

EXERCISE 287: Answer the following questions, which contain words from Essays 26 to 30.

1. Do you associate danger with a jungle?
2. Do you think that children need discipline?
3. Is a blues song usually about happy things?
4. Does a teacher expect a composition to be a student's individual work?
5. Is a law passed by the government the result of a sequence of actions?
6. Do you have a good deal of housework?
7. Is it possible that speakers of two different languages may disagree on whether a tune is melodic or not?
8. Are you restrained at times from saying what you want to by the necessity of being polite?
9. Does an actor know that he will necessarily spend a lot of time memorizing roles?
10. When do you customarily get a foundation lecture in school—at the beginning of a term or at the end?
11. Does a playwright sometimes interpolate a song between two scenes?
12. Do you agree with the quotation "Variety is the spice of life"?
13. Do the oceans contain a profuseness of marine life?
14. When you go to a professional performance, do you expect the actors to have rehearsed their roles?
15. Which would probably prefer to dance to swing music—young people or old?
16. Is breath basic to speech?
17. Can you anticipate roughly what the weather will be next month?
18. On which side of a conductor does the violin section of an orchestra usually sit?
19. Why would a fireman need to develop flexibility in his sleeping schedule?
20. What is the difference between "the former president" and the "late president"?
21. Is a symphony a polyrhythmic composition?
22. Is Beethoven now considered a classical composer?

23. Does the effect of a kind act depend to a great extent on its spontaneity?
24. Is the harmonic structure of a symphony relatively simple?
25. Do we all live within a framework of customs?
26. Does a cold sometimes bring about complications such as influenza and pneumonia?
27. How do you usually eliminate words in a composition?
28. Can friendship be considered the cement of a group?
29. Why do students tend to take the same seats at every meeting of a class?
30. Does an adviser point out paths that a person may follow?
31. Must an orchestra have a combination of instruments?
32. Who would customarily use subtle ways to express disagreement—a diplomat or a sergeant?
33. Would a completely skeptical person believe that something existed if he had not seen it?
34. Do adjectives usually fall behind nouns in English?
35. How do you feel when the answer to a question on an examination eludes you?
36. Does a performer want his audience to like him?
37. When you pass a bakery, do you sometimes smell a tantalizing aroma?
38. Where do you look up definitions?
39. Are some kinds of fairy stories enjoyed by adults and children alike?
40. When you first heard a native speaker of English, was his speech baffling to you?
41. Can a textbook be thought of as a key to knowledge?
42. Do you find it easy to keep your mind on something that is uninteresting?
43. Is a person from a small town frequently bewildered by the traffic in a large city?
44. Would a person who cared nothing about music be able to appreciate opera?
45. Is an advertising man concerned with the creation of desire for the products he is trying to sell?
46. What effect does kerosene have on a fire?
47. Is the maintenance of supplies crucial to an army in time of war?

48. What shape does a clarinet have?
49. Do children ask many questions of their mothers and fathers?
50. Is the beating of waves on a shore rhythmic on a calm day?
51. Would you understand what a person meant if he said that a trombone reminded him of a lot of plumbing?
52. Would you consider hunger to be a driving force?
53. How many people make up a quartet?
54. Do you sometimes scratch the top of your head to indicate that you are puzzled?
55. Does looking after her family constitute a full-time job for the average mother?
56. Do you sometimes become so absorbed in a book that you are scarcely aware of where you actually are?
57. Are musical notes distinguished by their unique quality?
58. Do you hope that ultimately the world will be at peace?
59. Is chamber music played by an ensemble?
60. Is the order of groups marching in a parade usually pre-arranged?
61. Where is the Library of Congress?
62. Which is the takeoff point for an airplane—the place where it begins its flight or the place where it ends its flight?
63. When a pianist gives a concert, does he usually play improvisations?
64. Can you find your way around this city without the benefit of a map?
65. Would a musicologist be interested in things like harmony and melody?
66. Can you name two jazz musicians?
67. Could putting together certain tones produce displeasing harmony?
68. What is used on a farm to keep cattle within bounds?
69. Can you give a clear explanation of something that is elusive for you?
70. Do you have more than one set of friends?

EXERCISE 288: Write an essay on one of the questions in Exercise 287.

ESSAY 31 THE PLEASURES OF WRITING BIOGRAPHY

BY WILLIAM WORTHEN APPLETON

Literary research has often been condemned as mere drudgery, a test of the author's stamina, and sometimes the reader's as well. The validity of such criticism depends largely upon the author's own attitude towards his work, for true literary research can be invested with as much excitement as can be found in the most advanced scientific laboratory. The results of one's findings may not be as spectacular as those of the nuclear physicist, but the literary researcher, too, is dealing with the stuff of life.

Within himself the researcher must combine the imagination of the artist, the intuition of the detective, and the metabolism of the longshoreman. The search for materials and their slow piecing together will call for the skill of the archeologist. Let us take, for example, the problem of identifying a letter with the signature and address torn off. By whom was it written? To whom was it sent? Working from clues in the body of the letter, we must patiently sift a mountain of material for a few pertinent grains of fact. In themselves the isolated facts may mean very little. However, in biography the sum of the whole often amounts to more than the sum of the individual parts.

Perhaps we have the good luck to find a related letter in the British Museum; a newspaper clipping in a miscellaneous collection in the Folger Library in Washington gives us a second clue; a letter in an extra-illustrated volume in Harvard's Houghton Library miraculously resolves the identities of the correspondents. We have rescued a moment in time. We have identified Mrs. Y, at the end of her fortunes in London, off on a desperate and futile trip to Dublin. Perhaps she will never see Mr. X again. If we are lucky, we can bring into focus the tawdry furnished room in which she scribbles the agitated note.

Our background reading serves to fill out the scene. The post chaise leaves for Chester at nine o'clock in the morning. Ahead of her is a two days' journey over snowy and gutted roads and after that, still worse, a plunging boat trip between Holyhead and Dublin Harbor. No wonder that her pen bites into the paper and that her scrawl becomes increasingly agitated and intense. Suddenly she has become alive for us. The torn letter seems as urgent and as immediate as this morning's mail. We have had a taste of the true joy of biography. While the scientist in his laboratory explores the potentialities of life, the biographer is re-creating life itself.

EXERCISE 289: Pronounce the following words, emphasizing the stressed syllable by saying the vowel louder, longer, and higher in pitch than the other vowels.

A. Emphasize the first syllable of these words:

pleasures	piecing	extra	scribbles
writing	problem	illustrated	agitated
literary	letter	volume	background
often	signature	Harvard	reading
drudgery	written	Houghton	Chester
author's	working	rescued	morning
stamina	body	moment	journey
sometimes	patiently	Mrs.	over
reader's	mountain	fortunes	snowy
criticism	pertinent	London	gutted
largely	isolated	desperate	after
attitude	little	futile	plunging
laboratory	British	Dublin	Holyhead
findings	newspaper	never	harbor
nuclear	clipping	Mr.	wonder
physicist	Folger	lucky	paper
dealing	library	focus	suddenly
artist	Washington	tawdry	urgent
longshoreman	second	furnished	scientist

B. Emphasize the second syllable of these words:

biography	within	however	o'clock
condemned	himself	amounts	ahead
validity	combine	perhaps	between
depends	detective	related	become
upon	metabolism	museum	increasingly
invested	material	collection	intense
excitement	together	miraculously	alive
advanced	example	resolves	immediate
results	identify	explores	
spectacular	themselves	biographer	
again	identities	itself	

C. Emphasize the third syllable of these words:

scientific	archeologist	miscellaneous	re-creating
intuition	individual	correspondents	

D. Emphasize the fourth syllable of these words:

imagination   potentialities

EXERCISE 290:   Read Essay 31 aloud.

EXERCISE 291:   Answer the following questions on the basis of Essay 31.

1. What is the opinion of some people about literary research?
2. Is the researcher supposed to have great endurance?
3. Can literary research be exciting?
4. With what is the researcher concerned?
5. What qualities should the researcher have?
6. What was missing in the letter?
7. Was the writer a man or a woman?
8. Was the person to whom it was sent a man or a woman?
9. Does it take much work to identify the letter?
10. Is the letter itself important?

11. Where is a related letter found?
12. What is found in Washington?
13. What finally identifies the correspondents?
14. At the time of writing the letter, was the woman unfortunate?
15. Where was she going?
16. Was the woman going to see the man?
17. In what kind of room did she probably write the letter?
18. Did she spend much time writing the letter?
19. In what kind of conveyance was she going to Chester?
20. When was she leaving?
21. How long would the trip take over land?
22. What was the condition of the roads?
23. Would the woman go to sea?
24. How did she feel when she wrote the letter?
25. Knowing the background, do you become interested in the letter?
26. Does the writer seem real to you?
27. How does a biographer differ from a scientist?
28. Do you think you would like to do literary research?

EXERCISE 292:   Give an oral summary of Essay 31.

EXERCISE 293:   Write a summary of Essay 31.

EXERCISE 294:   Write the parts of Essay 31 that the teacher dictates.

EXERCISE 295:   Write a composition on a topic suggested by Essay 31.

EXERCISE 296:   Answer the following questions, which contain words from Essay 31.

1. Do you enjoy reading the biography of a famous man?
2. On whom does your success largely depend?
3. What do you have to combine to make bread?
4. Is a notebook part of a student's materials?

5. Does a public library seem to have a mountain of books?
6. How much money does the average person's weekly grocery bill amount to?
7. Have you ever extra-illustrated a book—that is, added to it some pictures from other sources?
8. Did a lot of people use to think that scientists' dreams to travel beyond the earth were futile?
9. Could a post chaise travel as fast as a modern bus?
10. Are a politician's speeches before election day usually intense?
11. Is education supposed to help you develop your potentialities?
12. When does a cook have to sift flour?
13. Why do big industrial companies have research departments?
14. Why must a photographer bring his subject into focus before he takes a picture?
15. What are some pertinent questions that a doctor asks you when you are ill?
16. Is a well-dressed woman likely to wear tawdry clothes?
17. What kinds of documents can prove your identity?
18. Which is usually cheaper to rent—a furnished room or an unfurnished one?
19. Is an unpaved road likely to become gutted after a heavy rain?
20. Is it usually easy to read a note that someone has scribbled?
21. Whose findings gave us the law of gravity?
22. When you guess something correctly, do you use your intuition?
23. How many regular correspondents do you have?
24. Have you ever got seasick on a plunging boat trip?
25. Do you think that actors probably keep newspaper clippings about themselves?
26. Does a photograph rescue a moment in time?
27. Do most mothers get agitated when their children get dangerously ill?
28. If you got a bad grade because you had not studied, would you understand what your teacher meant if he said, "No wonder"?
29. Does a married man get a taste of bachelorhood when his wife goes away on a visit?
30. Can disease affect your metabolism?
31. Was Napoleon at the end of his fortunes on St. Helena?
32. If you were planning to write about Africa in the fifteenth

century, would you have to do some background reading so that you could know about customs then?

33. Where do longshoremen work?
34. Do you like to go off on a trip on a moment's notice?
35. Would you like to take some trips to fill out your knowledge of this country?
36. Is it difficult to read the scrawl of a child who is just learning to write?
37. Is a clue important in solving a mystery?
38. Do you think you have within yourself the ability to be a great writer?
39. Is it wiser to plan for the future than to hope you will always be lucky?
40. What are some of the pleasures of your life?
41. Does a researcher have to deal with facts?
42. Have you ever accidentally torn a page of a book?
43. Have you discovered that the best way to resolve some difficulties is to work hard on them?
44. Do snowy mountains make a pretty scene for you?
45. Do people often condemn things that they do not like?
46. Is an archeologist primarily interested in modern culture?
47. Have you ever got a lot of money by mere chance?
48. What do you consider are some of the immediate problems of the world?
49. Where do you put your signature on a letter?
50. Is it a joy for you to get up early in the morning?

EXERCISE 297: Write an essay on one of the questions in Exercise 296.

ESSAY 32 DANIEL BOONE

Frontiersmen are known for their wanderlust. A native-born colonial American, Daniel Boone was one of the most peripatetic. Born in Pennsylvania in 1734, he is identified with the breed of pioneers who were inured from birth to a strenuous life which [1]_____ hardy endeavor and [2]_____. Boone was [3]_____ with the spirit of adventure and [4]_____ the hazards of the wilds rather than what he would have considered the [5]_____ of farming or storekeeping. His expertness in hunting for wild animals and living off the land stood him in good stead in his numerous expeditions of [6]_____ the new country and opening it up to settlers. He guided home seekers to sites in the vast forests and helped set up trading posts, but he never tarried long in one place. His journeys took him as far south, north, and west as Florida, Michigan, and Missouri in an era when those [7]_____ territories were uncharted regions infested with savage Indians and predatory animals. In the American Revolution he demonstrated his [8]_____ as a scout and [9]_____ escaped from captivity by the Indians and the British. Although he served in various political capacities, his abiding love was the wilderness.

Boone's name has become so entangled with legends that it is well-nigh impossible to [10]_____ his biography. Typical of the idealization of Boone is the eulogy to him in Lord Byron's long poem *Don Juan*, "... back-woodsman of Kentucky ... happiest amongst mortals anywhere...."

EXERCISE 298: For each numbered blank in Essay 32, provide the word or phrase which best completes the meaning of the sentence. Make your selection from the numbered groups, which correspond to the numbered blanks. These lists contain words that appeared in Essay 31.

1.	2.	3.	4.
sifted	stamina	scribbled	combined
called for	findings	torn off	dealt with
amounted to	clipping	invested	rescued

5.	6.	7.	8.
metabolism	exploring	nuclear	skill
drudgery	condemning	isolated	clue
post chaise	depending upon	futile	grain

9.	10.
largely	agitate
intensely	piece together
miraculously	plunge

EXERCISE 299: Pronounce the following words, emphasizing the stressed syllable by saying the vowel louder, longer, and higher in pitch than the other vowels.

A. Emphasize the first syllable of these words:

Daniel	opening	Indians	anywhere
wanderlust	settlers	predatory	sifted
native	guided	demonstrated	stamina
strenuous	seekers	British	findings
hardy	forests	various	clipping
spirit	trading	wilderness	scribbled
hazards	never	legends	rescued
rather	tarried	typical	drudgery
farming	journeys	eulogy	nuclear
keeping	Florida	Byron's	isolated
hunting	Michigan	poem	futile
animals	era	woodsman	largely
living	territories	happiest	
numerous	regions	mortals	
country	savage	agitate	

B. Emphasize the second syllable of these words:

frontiersmen	uncharted	become	combined
colonial	infested	entangled	metabolism
American	escaped	impossible	exploring
identified	captivity	biography	condemning
inured	although	Kentucky	depending
endeavor	political	amongst	intensely
adventure	capacities	amounted	
considered	abiding	miraculously	
Missouri	invested	together	

C. Emphasize the third syllable of these words:

Pennsylvania   pioneers   expeditions   revolution

D. Emphasize the fourth syllable of this word:

peripatetic

E. Emphasize the fifth syllable of this word:

idealization

EXERCISE 300:   Read Essay 32 aloud with the blanks filled in.

EXERCISE 301:   Be prepared to answer any questions on Essay 32 that the teacher may ask.

EXERCISE 302:   Give an oral summary of Essay 32.

EXERCISE 303:   Write a summary of Essay 32.

EXERCISE 304:   Write the parts of Essay 32 that the teacher dictates.

EXERCISE 305: Write a composition on a topic suggested by Essay 32.

EXERCISE 306: Answer the following questions, which contain words from Essays 31 and 32.

1. What kind of work would you call drudgery?
2. Is a race a test of the runners' stamina?
3. Have doctors succeeded in isolating the cause of the common cold?
4. Does a person have to make a long search to find a place to live in this city?
5. Is it difficult to piece together a letter that has been torn to little bits?
6. Do men sometimes go exploring at the bottom of the sea?
7. Is the President of the United States invested with much power?
8. Have you ever thought that you had miraculously escaped from some bad accident?
9. Does a mountain climber need much skill?
10. Is there a grain of truth in some legends?
11. During the fall here, do the nights become increasingly long?
12. Does a biography deal with facts?
13. Are valuable things kept in a museum?
14. Did you receive any letters in this morning's mail?
15. Did the discovery of atomic energy bring about spectacular results?
16. Do many police departments employ detectives?
17. How much value does a piece of money have in itself?
18. Is a nuclear physicist interested in atoms?
19. Has a laundry ever torn off a sleeve of one of your shirts?
20. Do you have a box at home in which you keep miscellaneous things?
21. Have you ever got so agitated that when you wrote, your pen bit into the paper?
22. If a person tells a lie, does his statement have any validity?
23. What does a biologist deal with?
24. Where do you put the addressee's name on a letter?

25. Does a scientist form a theory from the sum of several experiments?
26. Do any of your friends have a stamp collection?
27. Do scientists sometimes have explosions in their laboratories?
28. Can criticism be helpful?
29. Do you like an author who gives you a lot of description so that you can visualize the scene of an action?
30. Does a sculptor have to work patiently?
31. Do you feel desperate when something pleasant has just happened to you?
32. Why should students have a good attitude toward homework?
33. Do the students in this room have individual seats?
34. Are you planning to leave for another country soon?
35. Does a novelist try to make his characters seem alive to his readers?
36. What does a biographer do?
37. What are some of the materials used for clothes?
38. Are there many parts in a wristwatch?
39. Do you think any remarkable inventions are ahead of us?
40. Do you sometimes re-create scenes of your childhood in your mind?
41. Does teaching call for a lot of patience?
42. Was Shakespeare a literary genius?
43. What is the most advanced scientific discovery you can think of?
44. Does a good storyteller have to have imagination?
45. Did you have the good luck to be healthy during the whole of last winter?
46. Does a doctor often receive urgent calls for help?
47. Do chemists work in laboratories?
48. Is a famous pianist sometimes called an artist?
49. Is biology related to chemistry to a great extent?
50. What frontiersmen can you think of?

EXERCISE 307: Write an essay on one of the questions in Exercise 306.

ESSAY 33 ERUDITE VILLAGE
BY SANFORD C. KAHRMANN

Although the United States government did not foresee and correctly estimate every one of its post-World War II problems, it showed careful thought in planning for the readjustment of its returning military personnel to civilian life. The GI Bill of Rights, Public Law 345, was the major governmental instrument provided by Congress and guided by the Veterans Administration to ease the readjustment. Among other benefits, a period of education at any level was offered, its length depending on the length of the veteran's military service.

As a consequence, returning soldiers, sailors, marines, and fliers headed toward colleges and universities at the beginning of 1946, almost as soon as they could get home from a separation center. By September of that year the flood of GI enrollments was reaching its crest. The schools responded excellently: Every qualified ex-serviceman entered the school of his choice and began his studies.

In many sections of the country a secondary problem accompanied the rush for education: student housing. Besides tuition and books, the GI bill gave a subsistence allowance which ranged in the beginning from $65 to $105 a month. The allowance was at best inadequate, even for the most farsighted and parsimonious student. There were some fortunate enough to be living with their parents. However, the large majority were themselves married and the heads of growing families. Once again the Federal government acted to ease the strain. The Public Housing Administration, a quasi-welfare bureau, began to arrange for low-cost housing where it could be made easily available near large university campuses. For the New York City universities—notably Columbia but also New York University and City College—the rusting sword of Camp Shanks was beaten into the plowshare of Shanks Village.

The village of Orangeburg, N.Y., lies a few miles west of the Hudson River and about 20 miles north of the New Jersey end of the George Washington Bridge. It has an industry—a factory producing fiber drainpipes—and it is served by two railroads and one bus line. The town consists largely of the Orangeburg School District. At the start of the war Orangeburg's population totaled 400.

Camp Shanks was built there, its warehouses along the West Shore Railroad, its barracks and administration buildings to the west of the tracks. Half a million or more soldiers passed through it on their way to or from Europe during the war. Their brief stay at the camp was spent in one-story, one-room barracks, each sleeping eighty or a hundred men. The barracks were heated by coal-burning pot-bellied stoves; toilet facilities were in separate outbuildings. A year after the end of hostilities the barracks were being converted into garden apartments.

Late in 1946 the first newcomers moved into their apartments, some of which were still incompletely converted. By the spring of 1947 conversion was nearly finished, and about two thousand families were living in the newly created Shanks Village. At its peak the population was 7,000, consisting of 2,800 families.

Rents were low. They ranged from $31 to $45 a month and included gas, water, and electricity. To accommodate a population that was expected to have a low income and to remain only a few years, furniture could be rented from the Public Housing Administration at comparably low cost.

Apartments were classified by the number of bedrooms and assigned according to the size of the family, from one bedroom for childless couples to three bedrooms for families with several children. Since the village was owned and managed by a Federal agency, there were none of the usual problems of local government. A man could devote his entire time to three activities: studying, acting like a father, and supplementing his subsistence allowance.

Thus, in that backwater hamlet began to evolve a pattern of communal living. An ingenious car pool overcame the difficulties of inadequate transportation and an uncooperative bus company. Baby-sitting pools—with membership limited and long lists of membership candidates—were organized. The Shanks Village Residents Association was formed to handle the community problems that were unrelated to housing. It promoted holiday dances and used-clothing sales. The whole business of living took on a unique economic design. The design was aimed at building family and community life while using the least possible amount of money, and it aimed to do those things within the structure of a vigorous capitalistic state.

As the men finished their undergraduate studies and went on to graduate work, many of them taught at their own or other schools. Frequently both husband and wife were studying for advanced degrees. One family achieved two Ph.D.'s and four children during their five-year residence. All six of them later became members, in their respective capacities, of the public school system of a New Jersey city. Shanks Village almost certainly had a heavier concentration of highly educated adults than any comparable area in the country.

Notice was served in 1954 that the Village was to cease operating. Already the population had been falling off as more and more families reached their educational goal and moved off to professional careers. Although the notice came suddenly and was worded clearly, governmental action was not hasty. Through 1955 and into 1956 several hundred families continued to live on the old terms in the Village apartments, but their number shrank steadily, and, in fact, the Village was gone.

The area today is bisected by the new parkway running from the George Washington Bridge to Bear Mountain State Park. The old barracks have been demolished. As fast as the debris could be burned and buried, a real estate development of 2,000 houses was built for sale. At the eastern edge of the former campsite stands the new Orangeburg Grammar School. It was built at government expense and donated, along with 15 or 20 acres of land, to the hamlet of Orangeburg so that the swarm of Shanks children would not overrun and overtax the old Orangeburg school.

When the new houses were finished and occupied, the change from an old to a new society was complete in Orangeburg. In less time than it takes a man to grow to voting age, the sleeping countryside was covered with an army camp; then, the shuffle of marching feet gave way to the rustle of school books and the nightly clack of typewriters; and now the voice of the home-owner is heard in the land, cheerful in the face of a monthly mortgage payment. How many spots of ground have served such varied functions as that small tract of land called Shanks?

EXERCISE 308: Pronounce the following words, emphasizing the stressed syllable by saying the vowel louder, longer, and higher in pitch than the other vowels.

A. Emphasize the first syllable of these words:

erudite	growing	thousand	residence
village	families	newly	later
government	federal	seven	members
estimate	acted	water	system
every	quasi	income	certainly
problem	welfare	only	heavier
careful	bureau	furniture	highly
planning	easily	rented	educated
military	campuses	comparably	comparable
public	notably	classified	area
major	also	number	notice
government	rusting	bedrooms	operating
instrument	beaten	childless	falling
Congress	into	couples	suddenly
veteran	plowshare	several	worded
other	Orangeburg	children	clearly
benefits	Hudson	managed	action
period	river	usual	hasty
any	twenty	local	steadily
level	Jersey	studying	parkway
offered	Washington	acting	running

military	industry	father	mountain
service	factory	supplementing	buried
consequence	fiber	backwater	eastern
soldiers	railroad	hamlet	former
sailors	largely	pattern	grammar
fliers	district	difficulties	acres
headed	totaled	company	occupied
agency	hundred	baby	voting
college	warehouses	sitting	countryside
center	barracks	membership	covered
reaching	buildings	limited	army
excellently	million	candidates	shuffle
qualified	Europe	organized	marching
serviceman	during	residents	rustle
entered	sleeping	handle	nightly
studies	eighty	holiday	typewriters
many	heated	dances	owner
sections	burning	clothing	cheerful
country	bellied	business	monthly
secondary	toilet	using	mortgage
student	separate	possible	payment
housing	after	money	guided
even	being	structure	varied
fortunate	garden	vigorous	functions
living	newcomers	graduate	
parents	nearly	frequently	
married	finished	husband	

B. Emphasize the second syllable of these words:

although	allowance	created	advanced
united	inadequate	consisting	degrees
foresee	enough	included	achieved
correctly	however	accommodate	became
returning	majority	expected	respective
civilian	themselves	remain	capacities
provided	again	assigned	already
among	arrange	according	professional
depending	available	devote	careers
marines	Columbia	entire	continued

beginning	about	activities	bisected
September	producing	evolve	demolished
enrollments	consists	ingenious	estate
responded	along	community	expense
began	facilities	promoted	society
accompanied	hostilities	unique	complete
besides	converted	design	
tuition	apartments	amount	
subsistence	conversion	within	

C. Emphasize the third syllable of these words:

readjustment	parsimonious	transportation	concentration
personnel	population	uncooperative	educational
education	incompletely	unrelated	overrun
university	electricity	economic	overtax
separation	overcame	undergraduate	

D. Emphasize the fourth syllable of these words:

administration   capitalistic

EXERCISE 309: Read Essay 33 aloud.

EXERCISE 310: Answer the following questions on the basis of Essay 33.

1. Did the United States foresee all the problems that would arise after World War II?
2. Did it correctly guess how great all those problems would be?
3. Was the government sensible about helping veterans after the war?
4. Why would veterans have to readjust after the war?
5. What was the most important law for veterans' readjustment?
6. Who passed that law?
7. Which agency carried out the provisions of that law?
8. What was one of the benefits of that law?
9. Could a veteran go to high school under the law?

10. Could a veteran go to school indefinitely and get the benefits?
11. Did many veterans accept those benefits?
12. Did it take them long to start to go to school?
13. When was there the largest number of veteran enrollments?
14. How did the schools react to the increased enrollments?
15. Did the schools take all the veterans who could go to school?
16. What particular problem did most of the veterans have?
17. What three things did the law provide for the veterans?
18. Was the allowance enough for living expenses?
19. As far as living expenses were concerned, which were the lucky veterans?
20. Which were the most unlucky veterans?
21. Were many of the veterans married?
22. Did any of them have children?
23. What was the Public Housing Administration?
24. What did it do to help the veterans?
25. Where did the Administration provide housing?
26. What was the name of the place where the New York City veterans went to live?
27. What had its name been?
28. What is the location of Orangeburg, N.Y.?
29. What industry does the town have?
30. What transportation facilities does it have?
31. What district is the town in?
32. At the beginning of World War II, what was the town's population?
33. What was the name of the army camp that was built there?
34. Where were the camp's warehouses situated?
35. Where were the barracks and the administration buildings?
36. How many soldiers went to the camp during the war?
37. What were their destinations?
38. Did a soldier stay at the camp long?
39. Where did the soldiers stay at the camp?
40. How many soldiers slept in a barracks?
41. What were the heating facilities in the barracks?
42. Where were the toilets?
43. What were the barracks used for after the war?
44. How long after the war did they start being converted?
45. When did families begin moving into the apartments?

46. Were all the apartments completely ready at first?
47. When were nearly all of the apartments ready?
48. How many families were living in the village in the spring of 1947?
49. What was the largest number of persons living there?
50. How many families were there at that time?
51. Was rent high for the apartments?
52. What was the range of rents?
53. What was included in the rent?
54. Were the renters expected to be wealthy?
55. Were they expected to remain there a long time?
56. Could furniture be rented?
57. Was the rent for the furniture high?
58. How were the apartments classified?
59. How were they assigned?
60. How many bedrooms did a couple without children have?
61. How many bedrooms did a large family have?
62. Who owned the village?
63. Who managed the village?
64. Were there problems of local government?
65. What did the men in the village do?
66. Was Shanks Village in a progressive area?
67. Did the author consider it a large place?
68. Were neighbors friendly with one another there?
69. Did people share cars?
70. Was regular transportation adequate?
71. Did the bus line try to help the inhabitants?
72. Did neighbors look after one another's children?
73. Did people want to join the plan of looking after children in turn?
74. What did the Shanks Village Residents Association concern itself with?
75. What were some of its activities?
76. Was the village like other communities?
77. What was the aim of the community?
78. Did the inhabitants intend to spend a lot of money?
79. Did they want to change the ways of capitalism?
80. What did many of the men do after they got their B.A. or B.S. degrees?

81. Were many of the wives students?
82. What did one family do in five years?
83. Where did that family go later?
84. Was Shanks Village unusual because of the amount of education of its inhabitants?
85. When did the government announce the end of the village?
86. Was the population increasing at that time?
87. Why did families move away?
88. Was the village discontinued suddenly?
89. How long did a large number of families continue to remain there?
90. Did those families change their way of living while they remained?
91. Does a new highway run through Shanks Village now?
92. What has happened to the barracks?
93. What was done to the wreckage?
94. How many new houses were built?
95. Are those houses rented?
96. Where is the new school?
97. Who built the new school?
98. Does the school have much land around it?
99. Who owns the school?
100. Why was the school built?
101. Were there many children in Shanks Village?
102. How many different kinds of people lived in the area within twenty years?
103. Do the new owners have any debts?

EXERCISE 311: Give an oral summary of Essay 33.

EXERCISE 312: Write a summary of Essay 33.

EXERCISE 313: Write the parts of Essay 33 that the teacher dictates.

EXERCISE 314: Write a composition on a topic suggested by Essay 33.

EXERCISE 315: Answer the following questions, which contain words from Essay 33.

1. Who provided you with clothes when you were a baby?
2. When are people in a rush?
3. When does a person have to make readjustments?
4. Is a man who used to be a soldier called a veteran?
5. When does the temperature in the summer usually reach its crest?
6. Do you expect a teacher to be erudite?
7. Are you a civilian?
8. Is tuition very expensive these days?
9. Does iron rust?
10. Do policemen carry swords in this city?
11. What does the term *G.I.* refer to?
12. Can you foresee the future?
13. What is the difference between a sailor and a marine?
14. Did your parents give you an allowance when you were young?
15. Do farmers use plowshares?
16. Have you ever wanted to be a flier?
17. Who looked after your welfare when you were young?
18. Can iron be beaten into various shapes?
19. Where do you head for after this class?
20. Is a pot used for cooking?
21. Does a farsighted person make plans for the future?
22. Is a village a large town or a small town?
23. Does a hotel try to accommodate travelers?
24. Would you be flattered if someone said you were pot-bellied?
25. Do you have a stove in your bedroom?
26. Are there toilet facilities in this building?
27. Do most farms have outbuildings?
28. Does cotton have fibers?
29. Do you pay rent?
30. Do you depend on someone for your subsistence?
31. Do you have any drainpipes in your house?
32. Is London a backwater town?
33. Have you ever done any baby sitting?
34. Do you belong to any group in which membership is limited?

35. If a landlord raises the rent, do his tenants live on the old terms?
36. Has notice ever been served on you to leave a place?
37. Do many tribes have communal living?
38. What is your capacity in this group?
39. Does a conservative person usually have radical beliefs?
40. Is the number of people in the world shrinking?
41. Do you admire an ingenious story?
42. Are you a member of a car pool?
43. Is France a capitalistic state?
44. Do people in your hometown move off very frequently?
45. Why is the Empire State Building unique?
46. Is the United States bisected by the Mississippi River?
47. Have stagecoaches given way to busses?
48. When can you hear the rustle of leaves on trees?
49. Is there usually much debris after a massive explosion?
50. Does the clack of a typewriter disturb you late at night?
51. Would you describe a metropolis as a sleeping countryside?
52. Is there much wreckage after an earthquake?
53. Can you often hear the shuffle of feet in the corridors of a school building?
54. What can happen if you fail to make a payment on a mortgage?
55. Can you buy a house from a real estate agent?
56. Should a law be worded clearly?
57. Are old buildings sometimes demolished for new construction?
58. Do you admire highly educated people?
59. Do most apartments in a large city have space for a garden?
60. Were your parents childless?

EXERCISE 316:   Write an essay on one of the questions in Exercise 315.

ESSAY 34 THE NORTHMEN

B etween the eighth and eleventh centuries a [1]_____ of
invaders, noted for their ferocity and daring, [2]_____
Europe. The sudden appearance of the Northmen (or Norse-
men or Vikings) seems to have been due to the [3]_____ of
the [4]_____ of Scandinavia by an [5]_____ rapid overpopulation and to the attempt of King Harald of Norway to
subjugate the independent nobles of his land. Either as raiders
or conquerors, the warriors set up their [6]_____ as far east
as Russia, where, as the Varangians, they founded the first
Russian state, and as far west as Iceland and even, according
to the Icelandic sagas and certain scholars, North America,
which Leif Ericson is supposed to have visited some five
centuries before Columbus and dubbed Vinland or Wineland.
The Northmen [7]_____ the northern islands of Scotland
and harassed the [8]_____ of eastern and southern England,
where they were called the Danes. As Normans in northern
France, they took over vast [9]_____ of land, which came to
be known as Normandy. From there they reinvaded England
in the Norman Conquest and defeated the English king in 1066
in the Battle of Hastings. In the early part of the eleventh
century, bands of Norman adventurers appeared in southern
Italy and Sicily in the [10]_____ of the local nobles, whom
they at first aided in their rebellion against Greek rule but later
dispossessed of their holdings. The Normans' continuing ambi-
tious plans against the Byzantine Empire during the Crusades
led them to their farthest excursion southeastward.

EXERCISE 317: For each numbered blank in Essay 34, provide the word
or phrase which best completes the meaning of the sentence. Make
your selection from the numbered groups, which correspond to the
numbered blanks. These lists contain words that appeared in Essay 33.

1.	2.	3.	4.
swarm	donated	clack	rustle
parkway	consigned	bisecting	hamlets
wreckage	overran	overtaxing	disks

5.	6.	7.	8.
indolently	bears	buried	shuffle
acridly	camp sites	occupied	debris
increasingly	mortgages	splashed	countryside

9.	10.
tracts	midst
barracks	sawdust
retinas	starch

EXERCISE 318: Pronounce the following words, emphasizing the stressed syllable by saying the vowel louder, longer, and higher in pitch than the other vowels.

A. Emphasize the first syllable of these words:

Northmen	Russia	southern	during
centuries	founded	England	farthest
noted	Russian	Norman	parkway
daring	Iceland	over	wreckage
Europe	even	Normandy	donated
sudden	sagas	conquest	rustle
Norsemen	certain	English	hamlets
Vikings	scholars	battle	indolently
rapid	Ericson	Hastings	acridly
Harald	visited	early	mortgages
Norway	Vinland	local	buried
subjugate	Wineland	Italy	occupied
nobles	northern	Sicily	shuffle
either	islands	aided	countryside
raiders	Scotland	later	barracks
conquerors	harassed	holdings	retinas
warriors	eastern	empire	sawdust

B. Emphasize the second syllable of these words:

between	according	adventurers	excursion
eleventh	Icelandic	appeared	southeastward
invaders	America	rebellion	consigned
ferocity	supposed	against	bisecting
appearance	before	continuing	increasingly
attempt	Columbus	ambitious	
Varangians	defeated	Crusades	

C. Emphasize the third syllable of these words:

Scandinavia	reinvaded	overran
independent	dispossessed	overtaxing

D. Emphasize the fifth syllable of this word:

overpopulation

EXERCISE 319:   Read Essay 34 aloud with the blanks filled in.

EXERCISE 320:   Be prepared to answer any questions on Essay 34 that the teacher may ask.

EXERCISE 321:   Give an oral summary of Essay 34.

EXERCISE 322:   Write a summary of Essay 34.

EXERCISE 323:   Write the parts of Essay 34 that the teacher dictates.

EXERCISE 324:   Write a composition on a topic suggested by Essay 34.

EXERCISE 325: Answer the following questions, which contain words from Essays 33 and 34.

1. Is your hometown a city or a village?
2. Do soldiers often live in camps?
3. Does Europe lie west of South America?
4. Are towns classified by the number of their inhabitants?
5. Is Paris a hamlet?
6. What is the size of the tract of land that this building occupies?
7. Why do some farmers keep a swarm of bees?
8. Has an invading army ever overrun this country?
9. Are you a former resident of Berlin?
10. Did you see any of your friends on your way to class?
11. Is a businessman concerned with economic matters?
12. Can you name a low-cost car?
13. When you are sick, do you usually feel that you are fortunate?
14. What animal is used to guide people?
15. Have any of your friends ever been in service in any army?
16. Do you try to respond when somebody asks you for help?
17. Can you estimate your living expenses?
18. Does a country have many postwar problems?
19. Have you ever worked in a government bureau?
20. Is your hometown served by a railroad?
21. Is November late in the year?
22. Would you like to move into a new house?
23. Is Asia north of Africa?
24. Do you think all industries will make a conversion to atomic power?
25. For whom was the George Washington Bridge named?
26. Would you like to devote your entire time to reading?
27. How can a teacher supplement his income?
28. What does the atmosphere of the earth consist of?
29. Are houses sometimes converted into apartments?
30. Is food unrelated to living?
31. Is the population of New York comparable to that of London?
32. Is housing adequate in your community?
33. Is there a river in this area?
34. What can a man do to build a happy family life?

35. Do bricks in a building usually form a pattern?
36. Do you spend the least possible amount of time on your studies?
37. Can you read steadily for several hours?
38. What may cause a company to cease operating?
39. What do you do with your used clothing?
40. Are you a resident in a hotel?
41. Have you reached your educational goal yet?
42. Does the sky usually take on a red color in the morning?
43. Is transportation in this city adequate?
44. When does a person become an adult?
45. Are you in grammar school right now?
46. How long have you occupied your present residence?
47. What are some of the benefits of marriage?
48. Do stage plays put on a nightly performance?
49. Are barracks usually as comfortable as hotels?
50. How long does it take a child to grow to manhood?
51. Have you seen any new real estate developments recently?
52. Do you find restaurants here and there in this city?
53. How do you feel in the face of danger?
54. Do you receive a monthly salary?
55. Can a person get sick if he overtaxes his strength?
56. Do soldiers have to do much marching?
57. Where is the financial center of the United States?
58. Is housing easily available in this city?
59. Are the majority of the people in this class men?
60. Who manages the money in your family?

EXERCISE 326: Write an essay on one of the questions in Exercise 325.

ESSAY 35 NURSERY RHYMES

Nursery rhymes are short poems and songs used in the
nursery and in games of children. Their content [1]———
from nonsense to thinly disguised sermonizing by the
[2]——— of families. Like proverbs, there is an appropriate
rhyme for every individual—for the generous child who is
thoughtful of others as well as for the [3]——— tot who
believes that having is better than giving. Some rhymes are
employed to [4]——— the strain of getting rebellious offspring to bed, and others are used in "counting out" games—
for instance, "Eenie, meenie, minie, mo." A [5]——— of
examples dates from the seventeenth century.

Most English nursery rhymes—[6]——— "Jack and Jill,"
"Simple Simon," and "Little Jack Horner"—have been
ascribed to Mother Goose. The originator of that personal
name was apparently not [7]——— enough to leave a written
explanation of it; as a [8]———, the origin is a matter of
dispute. Some derive it from a French collection of tales by
Charles Perrault (1697) which had the subtitle *Tales of
Mother Goose*. That name has in turn been traced to Queen
Goosefoot, the mother of Charlemagne and a patron of children. Others [9]——— the claim of an American source in
Mother Goose's Melodies, published in Boston in 1719 by
Thomas Fleet, whose mother-in-law was said to be Elizabeth
Vergoose. The subject matter of the rhymes has been
[10]——— by some scholars to actual events in English
political history.

EXERCISE 327: For each numbered blank in Essay 35, provide the word
or phrase which best completes the meaning of the sentence. Make
your selection from the numbered groups, which correspond to the
numbered blanks. These lists contain words that appeared in Essays
31 to 34.

1.	2.	3.	4.
ranges	marines	optional	ease
paraphrases	instruments	parsimonious	foresee
curbs	heads	fathomless	glare

5.	6.	7.	8.
pivot	notably	luxuriant	crest
harmonica	indigenously	inadequate	consequence
flood	restlessly	farsighted	rush

9.	10.
estimate	rusted
promote	etched
guide	related

EXERCISE 328: Pronounce the following words, emphasizing the stressed syllable by saying the vowel louder, longer, and higher in pitch than the other vowels.

A. Emphasize the first syllable of these words:

nursery	getting	written	history
poems	offspring	origin	ranges
children	counting	matter	paraphrases
content	instance	subtitle	instruments
nonsense	eenie	Goosefoot	optional
thinly	meenie	Charlemagne	fathomless
sermonizing	minie	patron	pivot
families	century	Goose's	notably
proverbs	English	melodies	restlessly
generous	simple	published	sighted
thoughtful	Simon	Boston	consequence
others	little	Vergoose	estimate
having	Horner	subject	rusted
better	mother	scholars	
giving	personal	actual	

B. Emphasize the second syllable of these words:

disguised	ascribed	Perrault	harmonica
appropriate	originator	American	indigenously
individual	apparently	Elizabeth	luxuriant
believes	enough	events	inadequate
employed	dispute	political	promote
rebellious	derived	marines	related
examples	collection	foresee	

C. Emphasize the third syllable of these words:

explanation   parsimonious

EXERCISE 329: Read Essay 35 aloud with the blanks filled in.

EXERCISE 330: Be prepared to answer any questions on Essay 35 that the teacher may ask.

EXERCISE 331: Give an oral summary of Essay 35.

EXERCISE 332: Write a summary of Essay 35.

EXERCISE 333: Write the parts of Essay 35 that the teacher dictates.

EXERCISE 334: Write a composition on a topic suggested by Essay 35.

EXERCISE 335: Answer the following questions, which contain words from Essays 31 to 35.

1. Will some medicine ease a headache?
2. Do you feel a strain when you have been working very hard?

3. Does a farsighted person make plans for the future?
4. Are there several children in your family?
5. Is a parsimonious person likely to give you some money?
6. Is there a flood of students at colleges in the fall?
7. Who is the head of your family?
8. Does a businessman try to promote his company's products?
9. Does knowledge come as a consequence of studying?
10. Do you know a growing industry?
11. What benefits does a person get from education?
12. What is your major interest in life?
13. What is another word for *ex-serviceman?*
14. What is the profession of your choice?
15. Is your supply of money absolutely inadequate?
16. Could you call a language an instrument?
17. Have you ever been offered a job?
18. Is this a one-story building?
19. What does your life largely consist of these days?
20. What does the population of your hometown total?
21. Were the first trains coal-burning?
22. Is a person wealthy if he has a low income?
23. Why does a large department store need a warehouse?
24. Do you feel that your education is still incomplete?
25. Is New Jersey near New York?
26. Is furniture very expensive these days?
27. Does your hometown have local government?
28. Have you ever slept in a barracks?
29. Can you think of any newly created nations?
30. Have you ever worked in an industry?
31. When is traffic at its peak in this city?
32. What is a factory used for?
33. Do you wish there could be an end to all hostilities?
34. Are you assigned a room when you register at a hotel?
35. Have you ever passed through Chicago?
36. What is the size of your family?
37. Is there a bus company in this city?
38. Do most people want a pleasant design of living?
39. Were you ever taught in a school?
40. Are you sometimes ashamed of a hasty action?
41. Do you have to earn your living?

42. Are you aiming at getting an important job?
43. What are some advanced degrees?
44. What characteristics do you think it desirable for a teacher to have?
45. Do you know several hundred people in this city?
46. What can evolve from an argument?
47. Do you regard a stupid person favorably?
48. Do you hope to achieve a well-paying job?
49. How many persons does your household consist of?
50. Do you make out a list for your laundry?
51. When is the next holiday?
52. What is the length of your residence in this city?
53. Is a scholar supposed to be intellectual?
54. Have you ever been a candidate for political office?
55. Do you enjoy going to dances?
56. Have you ever organized an association?
57. Does a company have a structure?
58. What is your capacity in this class?
59. Is merchandise usually cheaper at a sale than at other times?
60. Can you name a vigorous sport?
61. How can many difficulties be overcome?
62. When was the United Nations formed?
63. Is there a heavy concentration of office workers in a city?
64. What international agency helps people who are in trouble?
65. What kind of man handles legal problems?
66. Have you finished your undergraduate studies?
67. Are you planning to have a professional career?
68. Do you like uncooperative people?
69. Are accommodations good in a slum area?
70. What do you find on a camp site?
71. Is this a temporary building?
72. Have you ever made a change from one country to another?
73. Does the equator run from the North Pole to the South Pole?
74. Can you read a book in less time than it takes the author to write it?
75. Have you ever accidentally burned your clothing?
76. Have you ever donated money to a charity?
77. Have you ever buried any treasure?
78. Does this building cover an acre of land?

79. Are you a homeowner?
80. Are you in the midst of your classmates right now?
81. Were you born in a hamlet?
82. Are you cheerful when somebody tells you bad news?
83. Have you ever built a house?
84. Is this area covered with private homes?
85. Is your home for sale?
86. Who stays in an army camp?
87. Are the pyramids in Africa examples of new construction?
88. Are we at the eastern edge of this city?
89. Do you have to pay money on a mortgage?
90. Are there a dozen people in this room?
91. On what basis do you judge that a book is good?
92. Was the range of temperature very great yesterday?
93. Does a community usually make laws for itself?
94. What is the length of a day?
95. Do farmers depend on rain?
96. Did you accompany anybody to class today?
97. Are there many advertisements in the newspapers?
98. What word is used as the opposite of *military?*
99. Is your present housing adequate for your needs?
100. Will heat make ice melt?

EXERCISE 336: Write an essay on one of the questions in Exercise 335.

ESSAY 36 THE QUEEN'S WITTY GODSON
BY ELIZABETH STORY DONNO

Born *circa* 1561, John Harington—the poet, courtier, soldier, epigrammatist, and letter writer—owed much of his privileged status to the experiences of his parents during the turbulent years before Queen Elizabeth I's accession. His mother, who had been a gentlewoman attendant of Princess Elizabeth, and his father both suffered reprisals because of their loyalty and service to the future queen, but as a consequence they gained a royal godmother for their first child.

"Boy Jack," as the queen affectionately called him, was educated first at Eton and then at Cambridge, where, despite his later assertion that he had had as good conscience as others of his fellows to take but a little learning for his money, he acquired an excellent education. Having received his M.A. degree in 1581, he proceeded like other fashionable gentlemen to study law at an inn of court in London, a study curtailed by the death of his father in 1582. He then returned to the family estate at Kelston near Bath to take up his duties as a householder and landed proprietor. For the next few years he busied himself with his family and estate, but the stimulus and glitter of court life also attracted him, and he made periodic visits to London.

On one of those visits, according to tradition—a tradition supported by Harington's own remarks—he circulated his translation of a ribald canto of the *Orlando Furioso* among the queen's maids of honor. Although the queen herself heartily enjoyed a jest, she saw fit to banish her godson from court until he had translated the whole as a penance. As a result, his translation of Ariosto appeared in 1591 in a handsome folio with a dedication to the queen.

Haunted by "ambition's puffball" and the excitement of the court, Harington continued to visit London, where, according to a lifelong habit, he recorded amusing and satirical observations in a series of epigrams, epigrams that remained unpublished until after his death but which circulated among his friends and did much to establish his reputation as a wit. In 1596 he published a witty effusion entitled "A New Discourse of a Stale Subject Called the Metamorphosis of Ajax." Actually a tissue of social and political allusions with many telling if covert thrusts at the issues, figures, and scandals of the day, his literary effort resulted once again in his temporary retirement to Kelston.

In 1599 Harington participated in the war in Ireland, where he was knighted by the Earl of Essex. That unfortunate campaign, followed by the rebellion and execution of Essex in 1601, brought a dispirited change over queen and court. On his next visit Harington received a sharp rebuke: "Go tell that witty fellow, my godson, to get home; it is no season to fool it here." He returned to Kelston.

Although sincerely fond of the queen, Harington, like other courtiers, opportunistically looked to Scotland and to the prospective reign of James I. Consequently, in 1602 he made the gesture of sending the king a New Year's gift—Latin and English verses to delight that pedant's heart and a curious perfumed lantern decorated with symbolic figures and bearing the legend of the thief on the cross, "Lord, remember me when thou comest into thy kingdom."

During the last few months of the queen's life, Harington spent much time at court, hoping with his fooleries to elicit a smile from his dear queen and royal godmother. However, her death was near. Describing his emotions after his last visit with the queen, he told his wife that to have turned away with tearless eye would have fouled the spring and fount of gratitude.

EXERCISE 337: Pronounce the following words, emphasizing the stressed syllable by saying the vowel louder, longer, and higher in pitch than the other vowels.

A. Emphasize the first syllable of these words:

witty	loyalty	fashionable	heartily
godson	service	gentlemen	banish
Harington	future	study	penance
poet	consequence	London	handsome
courtier	royal	family	folio
soldier	godmother	Kelston	haunted
letter	educated	duties	puffball
writer	Eton	householder	lifelong
privileged	Cambridge	landed	habit
status	later	busied	series
parents	conscience	stimulus	epigrams
during	other	glitter	after
turbulent	fellow	also	published
mother	little	visit	discourse
gentlewoman	learning	circulated	subject
princess	money	ribald	Ajax
father	excellent	canto	actually
suffered	having	honor	decorated
tissue	effort	consequently	bearing
social	temporary	gesture	legend
many	Ireland	sending	comest
telling	knighted	Latin	kingdom
covert	Essex	English	hoping
issues	followed	verses	fooleries
figures	over	pedant's	tearless
scandals	season	curious	gratitude
literary	Scotland	lantern	

B. Emphasize the second syllable of these words:

experience	proprietor	excitement	campaign
before	himself	continued	rebellion
Elizabeth	attracted	recorded	dispirited
accession	according	amusing	received
attendant	tradition	satirical	rebuke
reprisals	supported	remained	returned
because	remarks	unpublished	sincerely

affectionately	translation	establish	prospective
despite	Orlando	effusion	delight
assertion	among	entitled	perfumed
acquired	although	political	remember
received	herself	allusions	symbolic
degree	enjoyed	resulted	elicit
proceeded	until	again	however
curtailed	result	retirement	describing
returned	appeared	participated	emotions
estate	ambition's	unfortunate	away

C. Emphasize the third syllable of these words:

epigrammatist	Furioso	observations	execution
education	Ariosto	reputation	
periodic	dedication	metamorphosis	

D. Emphasize the fourth syllable of this word:

opportunistically

EXERCISE 338: Read Essay 36 aloud.

EXERCISE 339: Answer the following questions on the basis of Essay 36.

1. In which century did Harington live?
2. What were his accomplishments?
3. What was his mother's function at court?
4. When and why was harm done to his parents?
5. What was the repayment to them for their loyalty?
6. Did his parents have more than one child?
7. What was the queen's nickname for Harington?
8. To which schools did he go?
9. In later years did he claim to have been an industrious student?
10. Was he well educated?
11. What degree did Harington obtain?

12. How old was he then?
13. Which profession did he begin to prepare for?
14. Was it stylish to study law?
15. What is the English equivalent of an American law school?
16. What caused Harington to cut short his course of study?
17. For what reason did he return home?
18. Did he stay on his estate most of the time in the next few years?
19. What drew him to London occasionally?
20. When did he let some gentlewomen read his partial translation of Ariosto?
21. What was the content of that translation?
22. Did the queen have a sense of humor?
23. What punishment did she impose on Harington?
24. When was his complete translation published?
25. What word did Harington use to refer to the insubstantiality of ambition?
26. Was he in the habit of writing epigrams?
27. What were they about?
28. Did anyone ever see them?
29. Were they considered very good?
30. What was the content of his "Metamorphosis of Ajax"?
31. Did the queen approve of that piece of writing?
32. Where did Harington go to war?
33. Who was his leader?
34. Was the campaign successful?
35. What happened to Essex?
36. What effect was there on the queen?
37. Did she welcome Harington on his next visit?
38. Who did he think would succeed Queen Elizabeth?
39. What did he send the king?
40. Was it probable that the king would like the gift?
41. Was Harington near the queen very much in the last few months of her life?
42. Did he cry the last time he saw her?
43. Was he grateful to the queen?

EXERCISE 340: Give an oral summary of Essay 36.

EXERCISE 341: Write a summary of Essay 36.

EXERCISE 342: Write the parts of Essay 36 that the teacher dictates.

EXERCISE 343: Write a composition on a topic suggested by Essay 36.

EXERCISE 344: Answer the following questions, which contain words from Essay 36.

1. Do you have a godson?
2. Was your great-grandfather a householder in this country?
3. In which language was the story of the original Ajax first told?
4. When might a child receive a sharp rebuke from his father?
5. How long ago did kings use to be entertained by the fooleries of court jesters?
6. Is a princess a royal person?
7. From what does a landed proprietor derive income?
8. Are you likely to find a ribald joke in dignified writing?
9. Is a folio a large or a small book?
10. Is a culture a tissue of customs?
11. Are most questions made to elicit a response from someone?
12. Would you describe our present era as turbulent?
13. Does a fashionable person follow current modes?
14. Is a canto made up of a few lines or many?
15. Would an utter foreigner easily understand allusions made to current events in a country?
16. Is toilet soap usually perfumed?
17. Was America discovered *circa* 1490?
18. Is there a ceremony at the accession of a king of England?
19. Is a maid of honor a married woman or a single woman?
20. If you have a guilty conscience, are you haunted by a good thing or a bad thing you have done?
21. Would a politician be interested in making telling remarks about his opponents?
22. Did you know that nowadays we would probably say "play the fool" instead of "fool it"?

23. Who would have more need of a lantern—a city dweller or a farmer?

24. In England is the term *gentlewoman* applied to any woman who has socially acceptable conduct?

25. Are some people convicted of crimes despite their assertions of innocence?

26. Do you think that many young people in small towns are attracted by what they consider to be the glitter of a metropolis?

27. Can ambition be an effective stimulus?

28. Would you be more likely to smile than laugh when you heartily enjoyed a laugh?

29. Would you expect an effusion from a talkative person or from a restrained person?

30. Would a government care if one of its covert agreements got published in a newspaper?

31. What is a man's title after he is knighted?

32. When a dear relative dies, does a woman usually turn away with a tearless eye?

33. Are there courtiers in the United States?

34. Would an argument be curtailed if one of the participants walked away?

35. What would you like to say to a person who brings up a stale subject?

36. Are political candidates given to making thrusts at their opposition?

37. Is an earl very high in rank?

38. Would a confidence man opportunistically be gracious to certain people?

39. Do you have any coins that bear legends?

40. Would you care if somebody fouled the city's water supply?

41. Would a conscientious student intend to take but a little knowledge in college?

42. Does a nation defeated in war expect to suffer reprisals?

43. Is it a good idea to make periodic visits to a doctor?

44. When would a parent see fit to punish a child?

45. Who customarily records the events of a conference?

46. What is one of the political issues of the day?

47. Is any nation currently making a campaign against another country?
48. To whom did you look for help when you were young?
49. Would you be pleased to have a thief as a friend?
50. Is an epigrammatist a clever person?
51. Would a beggar be likely to have a family estate?
52. Who can banish a criminal from society?
53. Are you flattered when somebody makes a satirical observation about your conduct?
54. When you go to a lecture, are you prepared for a discourse?
55. Are criminals usually hanged on a cross in this country?
56. Why is a university sometimes referred to as a fount of knowledge?
57. Would you be happy if somebody ordered your execution?
58. When an American uses the term *Lord,* to whom is he probably referring?
59. What was the nationality of Ariosto?
60. Which is the more complimentary term—*pedant* or *scholar?*

EXERCISE 345: Write an essay on one of the questions in Exercise 344.

ESSAY 37 METAMORPHOSIS

Insects such as beetles, flies, mosquitoes, gnats, moths, and butterflies undergo a series of radical changes in their structure before they [1]_____ their adult status. The process of transformation from egg to larva to pupa to adult is termed [2]_____. The most [3]_____ stage is that of the pupa. When the time comes for their entering that period, most moth larvae [4]_____ themselves secreting silk to spin an outer case called a cocoon. On the other hand, butterfly larvae usually attach their posterior end to a leaf, stem, or branch by a button of silk and quite abruptly [5]_____ to take on a hard covering called a chrysalis. A few pupae—for example, of the mosquitoes—are active, but as a rule in the pupa case the insect is in temporary [6]_____ from movement. Within the case occur the evolutional changes which [7]_____ the adult: Quiescent embryonic cells which have been carried by the larva receive the [8]_____ to multiply and absorb the larval tissue. In other words, the creature which emerges from the case [9]_____ its body and life to the different creature that entered the pupa. The time required for the pupa to [10]_____ its adult form varies with the species: for some insects, only a few days are needed; for others, a whole winter.

EXERCISE 346: For each numbered blank in Essay 37, provide the word or phrase which best completes the meaning of the sentence. Make your selection from the numbered groups, which correspond to the numbered blanks. These lists contain words that appeared in Essay 36.

1.	2.	3.	4.
haunt	glitter	curious	curtail
suffer	courtier	periodic	busy
acquire	metamorphosis	stale	reign

5.
banish
proceed
elicit

6.
canto
accession
retirement

7.
result in
take up
foul

8.
folio
stimulus
campaign

9.
owes
supports
accede

10.
gain
participate
fume

EXERCISE 347: Pronounce the following words, emphasizing the stressed syllable by saying the vowel louder, longer, and higher in pitch than the other vowels.

A. Emphasize the first syllable of these words:

insects	entering	temporary	species
beetles	period	movement	only
butterfly	larvae	carried	needed
series	outer	multiply	winter
radical	other	larval	glitter
changes	usually	tissue	curious
structure	button	creature	banish
status	covering	body	canto
process	chrysalis	different	folio
larva	pupae	entered	stimulus
pupa	active	varies	

B. Emphasize the second syllable of these words:

mosquitoes	abruptly	required	result
before	example	acquire	campaign
themselves	within	curtail	supports
secreting	quiescent	proceed	accede
cocoon	receive	elicit	participate
attach	absorb	accession	
posterior	emerges	retirement	

C. Emphasize the third syllable of these words:

metamorphosis   transformation   embryonic
undergo   evolutional   periodic

EXERCISE 348: Read Essay 37 aloud with the blanks filled in.

EXERCISE 349: Be prepared to answer any questions on Essay 37 that the teacher may ask.

EXERCISE 350: Give an oral summary of Essay 37.

EXERCISE 351: Write a summary of Essay 37.

EXERCISE 352: Write the parts of Essay 37 that the teacher dictates.

EXERCISE 353: Write a composition on a topic suggested by Essay 37.

EXERCISE 354: Answer the following questions, which contain words from Essays 36 and 37.

1. What is often a great stimulus to getting a job?
2. Was Napoleon's retirement to Elba temporary?
3. With what does a banker busy himself?
4. What does a comedian hope to elicit from his audience?
5. How long a study does a candidate for a Ph.D. usually have to make before acquiring his degree?
6. Would you want your children to acquire an excellent education?
7. Is electric lighting the culmination of a series of discoveries?
8. Would a very ugly girl be likely to wish for a metamorphosis?
9. Do you owe your education to yourself, to your parents, or to someone else?

10. Do you think a genius should have a privileged status?
11. Are you likely to gain friends by being rude?
12. Are rumors circulated very fast?
13. Do you know the century in which *Gulliver's Travels* first appeared?
14. Would you say that the efforts of the League of Nations resulted in permanent peace?
15. Are gifts supposed to delight the receiver's heart?
16. What is the name of the present ruler of England?
17. What does a student proceed to do when he finishes his premedical education?
18. Who would you say did much to establish the United Nations?
19. When would a rider tell his horse to get home?
20. Have you run across any curious customs recently?
21. Are you your parents' first child?
22. To whom do authors nowadays usually make their dedications?
23. Does a new doctor usually work very hard to establish a reputation?
24. Do you know in which world war General Pershing participated?
25. When is the season for oysters?
26. Do any of your friends affectionately call you by a name other than your legal one?
27. Is studying law a long process?
28. What is the capital of Ireland?
29. Is it unfortunate that most of us never know when death is near?
30. Do many parents hope that their children will be future presidents?
31. Are public buildings often decorated with symbolic figures?
32. To whom is an aide-de-camp an attendant?
33. Is English court life still characterized by ceremony?
34. What are you expected to do when somebody tells you a jest?
35. Is it easy to get rid of a lifelong habit?
36. Must most boys nowadays expect to be soldiers?
37. What is the book you are currently reading entitled?
38. Do a great number of rivers have their origin in a spring?

39. Is it logical for an employer to expect a degree of loyalty from his employees?

40. According to tradition, did William Tell shoot an apple off his son's head?

41. Who were some of the figures at the most recent international conference?

42. Has there ever been a rebellion in this country?

43. Who is usually the prospective ruler in a kingdom?

44. Are most people good letter writers, would you say?

45. Is a citizen supposed to render service to his country in time of war?

46. When did you take up your study of English?

47. Does an accusation in court have to be supported by evidence?

48. Have you read the whole of Cervantes' *Don Quixote?*

49. Do some newspapers seem to take delight in printing scandals?

50. When did the reign of Elizabeth II of England begin?

51. Would you feel gratitude toward a person who had done you a disservice?

52. Do you feel cheated if you receive a bad bargain for your money?

53. What are some of the duties of a mother?

54. Whose remarks are more likely to be repeated—a dull person's or a witty person's?

55. Are you pleased when you make an epigram?

56. Can you name one of the literary efforts of Poe?

57. When is a person given something to do as a penance?

58. Can rainy weather bring a dispirited change over you?

59. Where was Marie Antoinette during the last few months of her life?

60. What is the gesture that two men make when they are introduced to each other?

EXERCISE 355: Write an essay on one of the questions in Exercise 354.

ESSAY 38　INTRODUCTION TO SEAFARING

BY DANIEL B. DODSON

When I look back at it now, I cannot understand what induced me to go to sea. I do not like deep water, and I get seasick very easily. However, during the summer months boys of sixteen are likely to suffer from boredom and passionate, mysterious flashes of romanticism: That is the only possible explanation.

Since I was not a member of the Maritime Union, the only way I could get aboard a ship was through the company, and providentially my father had a friend who was president of a steamship company which operated out of Portland, Oregon (my home), into Oriental waters. Therefore, on one brilliant day in early June, I clambered aboard the *S.S. Texas*, 9,000 tons, bound west for the East, loaded with lumber.

Our departure was not auspicious. There was something wrong with the rudder. (I will confess right now that I have forgotten most of the nautical terminology I learned in those four months. I recall *fore* and *aft*, *starboard* and *port*, *above* and *below*, *forecastle* and *fiddley*, but the more recondite nomenclature escapes my memory entirely.) Since, in order to retain the mail contract, it was necessary for us to be away from the pier by midnight, at nine o'clock when the rudder still adamantly refused to function, a tug took us in tow, and we started cautiously down the Willamette River toward the Columbia River and the Pacific Ocean.

I never learned precisely what happened that night. I went to bed a little after 11:30 (as a cadet, a junior officer, I had an 8 by 4 cabin of my own.) I had been asleep about an hour when I was awakened by a great lurch and the traumatic sound of crushing, splintering timbers, which continued, it seemed, an unconscionably long time. Then, there was a profound vibrating shock and silence. I was prepared to abandon ship incontinently. It would have been quite simple to move unobtrusively to the port side, drop onto the pier which we had sundered, and catch a bus home. After thinking it over, however, I decided that it was probably a standard if somewhat flamboyant manner of leaving port, and I went back to sleep.

The next twenty-two days were the most unpleasant I had yet spent in my life. I was assigned to the Black Gang in the engine and boiler rooms. From the time we left the Columbia River until we entered Yokohama harbor, except for eating and sleeping, I was on my back under the floor plating of the engine room, lying in 6 inches of grease and water, trying to paint with red lead several hundred miles of hot steampipes. Upon emerging after the first day's work, I entered the petty officers' mess, and the boatswain, a choleric and pugnacious young man named Jenkins, told me that the sight of me made him sick and ordered me to my quarters to eat. I knew I was a pretty repulsive object, and it took me six months to get the red lead and grease out of my hair and off my skin. I heaved a huge sigh of relief when we sighted Japan, and even though I had not finished the job, nothing, not even the threat of death, would have compelled me to go back to the steam pipes. Fortunately, a very efficient gang of laborers was hired to do the job which I had started. They did it very well, and they did it in six hours.

I spent the day in Yokohama on shore leave much like any novice seaman, looking at the city and drinking beer. We were supposed to report back to the ship at 6 P.M., but when I returned at 5:30, I was taken aback to find only about half the crew on board and that half sprawled on decks, on hatches, and in companionways. By 6:30 all but three men had staggered aboard, but only about six were able to go on watch. At 7 the captain, an elderly Dane whose English was sinewy but limited, came out on the bridge and ordered the anchor lifted. The men were sullen. They knew that their three missing shipmates would catch the ship in Kobe, our next port of call, but they also knew that they would be under arrest by the Japanese police, that they would have to pay the train fare for themselves and for their escorts, and that their pay would be severely docked. The anchor came up to the water line, but then somebody cut off the steam to the winch. Simultaneously somebody cut the lines to the turbines in the engine room. We were adrift.

The captain bellowed some discouraging threats, but nobody moved. He sent the second mate dcwn to order us all to the forward deck, and a few minutes later he appeared there himself with a revolver stuck in his belt. I was not sure of the precise legal definition of mutiny, but this seemed to fulfill most of the qualifications I had read about.

The captain gave more commands, but still nobody moved. He argued piteously and threatened some more, rather wildly. If there had been a man-of-war in the harbor, he asserted, he would have had us all in chains. Looking us over with no enthusiasm, he descried Jenkins and ordered him to approach. Jenkins shouldered his way through the men, reeling marvelously. The captain opened his mouth to say something uncomplimentary, I suspect—but he never completed it. With one remarkably rhythmic staggering sway, Jenkins swung a long, whistling haymaker which caught the captain on the side of the head and sent him sprawling one way and his gun clattering another. Jenkins's heroism was brief. Somebody jumped on his back, and somebody else jumped on the jumper's back, and then I did not see what happened because somebody knocked me down. The minute I hit the deck I started crawling, since I had not yet had much experience in general brawls and since I was outweighed by everyone on the ship except the radio operator, whom I could not find. I crawled over the hatch and hid.

Happily, the ruckus did not last long, for by then we were perilously close to the lights of another ship. The second mate got hold of the captain's revolver and began blasting away at the sky. The reports woke up the first mate and the first engineer, and through their combined efforts the fight was stopped except between Jenkins and Chips, the carpenter, both of whom seemed to like to fight. They went on until Jenkins knocked Chips out.

The second mate, the only officer who was able to stay on deck, was the hero of the action. He got the anchor up and the turbines going again. Nevertheless, apparently even he was confused. When we woke up the next morning, we had started back to Portland. We were 75 miles east of Japan, and we had to turn around to continue our voyage through the Inland Sea and hence on to China and the Philippine Islands. In Kobe we picked up the three missing sailors, drunken, begrimed, bedraggled, and impenitent.

As I have said, I do not know what mysterious urge impelled me to go to sea. However, it had one practical result for which I am thankful. Later, when I had a choice, I chose the Air Force rather than the Navy. Airplanes do not have anchors. Besides, I do not get airsick.

EXERCISE 356: Pronounce the following words, emphasizing the stressed syllable by saying the vowel louder, longer, and higher in pitch than the other vowels.

A. Emphasize the first syllable of these words:

seafaring	function	choleric	rather
water	started	Jenkins	wildly
seasick	cautiously	quarters	shouldered
very	river	pretty	reeling
easily	toward	object	marvelously
during	ocean	sighted	opened
summer	never	finished	something
likely	happened	nothing	rhythmic
suffer	little	even	staggering
boredom	after	fortunately	whistling
passionate	thirty	laborers	haymaker
flashes	junior	novice	sprawling
only	officer	seaman	clattering
possible	cabin	looking	heroism

member
maritime
union
company
father
president
steamship
operated
Portland
Oregon
into
therefore
brilliant
early
clambered
Texas
loaded
lumber
something
rudder
nautical
starboard
forecastle
fiddley
nomenclature
memory
order
contract
necessary
midnight

crushing
splintering
timbers
vibrating
silence
simple
onto
sundered
thinking
over
probably
standard
somewhat
manner
leaving
twenty
engine
boiler
entered
harbor
eating
sleeping
under
plating
lying
inches
trying
several
hundred
petty

city
drinking
taken
hatches
staggered
captain
elderly
English
sinewy
limited
anchor
lifted
sullen
missing
shipmates
Kobe
also
escorts
somebody
turbines
bellowed
nobody
second
forward
minute
later
legal
mutiny
argued
piteously

jumper's
crawling
general
everyone
radio
operator
happily
ruckus
perilously
blasting
efforts
carpenter
hero
action
seventy
voyage
inland
China
Philippine
islands
sailors
drunken
practical
thankful
Navy
airplanes
airsick
threatened
boatswain
adamantly

B. Emphasize the second syllable of these words:

induced
however
mysterious
romanticism
aboard
departure

cadet
asleep
about
awakened
traumatic
continued

compelled
efficient
supposed
report
returned
aback

suspect
completed
remarkably
another
because
experience

auspicious	unconscionably	companionways	outweighed
confess	profound	arrest	began
forgotten	prepared	police	combined
recall	abandon	themselves	between
above	incontinently	severely	apparently
below	decided	adrift	confused
escapes	flamboyant	discouraging	around
entirely	unpleasant	appeared	continued
retain	assigned	himself	begrimed
away	until	revolver	bedraggled
o'clock	except	precise	impenitent
refused	upon	fulfill	impelled
Willamette	emerging	commands	result
Columbia	pugnacious	asserted	besides
Pacific	repulsive	enthusiasm	
precisely	relief	descried	
eleven	Japan	approach	

C. Emphasize the third syllable of these words:

introduction	providentially	unobtrusively	simultaneously
understand	Oriental	Yokohama	definition
explanation	terminology	Japanese	engineer

D. Emphasize the fourth syllable of these words:

qualifications   uncomplimentary   nevertheless

EXERCISE 357:   Read Essay 38 aloud.

EXERCISE 358:   Answer the following questions on the basis of Essay 38.

1. Does the author know why he became a sailor?
2. Does he like sailing?
3. Does he ever get seasick?
4. When do sixteen-year-old boys get bored?
5. Do they have feelings which are hard to explain?

6. Was the author a regularly employed seaman?
7. How did he manage to be hired?
8. What was his hometown?
9. To what part of the world did the company's ships go?
10. When did the author begin his job?
11. What was the name of the steamship?
12. How much did it weigh?
13. Where was it going?
14. What was its cargo?
15. Did the trip begin favorably?
16. What part of the equipment was defective?
17. Does the author remember a great number of the words used in shipping?
18. What are some of the terms that he remembers?
19. Have you ever seen or heard any of those words before?
20. What kinds of words has the author forgotten?
21. How long did the author's employment last?
22. When and why did the ship have to depart?
23. What happened at nine o'clock?
24. Where did the ship go?
25. Is it clear in the author's mind what occurred late in the night?
26. When did the author go to bed?
27. Did he have a large room?
28. Did he have any roommates?
29. What was his classification?
30. What woke him up?
31. What time was it when he awoke?
32. Do you think you would have enjoyed the sensation he got?
33. What did he first think of doing?
34. Why did he go back to sleep?
35. Did he enjoy his work for the next three weeks?
36. Did his work get him dirty enough to make the adjective *black* appropriate?
37. Where did his group work?
38. Did he have to work many hours a day?
39. What was his specific job?
40. Who would not let him eat with the petty officers?
41. Where did he have his meals?
42. Did the author realize that his appearance was not attractive?
43. How long did it take him to clean himself completely?

44. How did he feel when Japan came into view?
45. Did he finish his job?
46. Was he willing to finish it?
47. Who did finish the job?
48. How long did it take?
49. When the author got to Yokohama, did he act differently from any new sailor?
50. How long did he stay there?
51. What did he do there?
52. When did the sailors have to go back to the ship?
53. When did the author get back?
54. What was the author's emotion when he returned to the ship?
55. What was the cause of that feeling?
56. What was the matter with the sailors?
57. By when had almost all the sailors returned?
58. How many were sober?
59. What was the nationality of the captain?
60. Was he an old man or a young man?
61. Did he speak English like a native?
62. Did he customarily speak gently?
63. What command did he give?
64. Were the sailors in a good humor?
65. Were they afraid the three absent sailors would be left in Japan?
66. Would the three be found by the police?
67. Would they have to pay any money?
68. Would they lose part of their wages?
69. Was the anchor raised completely?
70. Why was it not taken on board?
71. Why was the ship out of control?
72. Did the captain express anger?
73. Did the sailors obey him?
74. Where did the second mate lead the sailors?
75. Did the captain have a gun?
76. Did it seem to the author that the sailors were revolting from their duty?
77. Did the captain ask the sailors to obey him?
78. Why did he mention a particular kind of ship?
79. Whom did he tell to come nearer?
80. Was Jenkins sober?

81. Did the captain start to say something to Jenkins?
82. Did Jenkins hit the captain?
83. Did everybody begin to fight?
84. Did the author get hit?
85. Why did he not fight back?
86. Did the commotion last long?
87. Was there any danger of hitting another ship?
88. Whose gun did the second mate get?
89. Did the second mate shoot at the men?
90. Who came to help the second mate?
91. Who were the last to stop fighting?
92. Who managed to get the ship in operation?
93. What mistake did he make?
94. Where did the ship go after Japan?
95. Where were the three missing sailors found?
96. How did they look?
97. Were they sorry for what they had done?
98. Why did the author go into the Air Force?

EXERCISE 359: Give an oral summary of Essay 38.

EXERCISE 360: Write a summary of Essay 38.

EXERCISE 361: Write the parts of Essay 38 that the teacher dictates.

EXERCISE 362: Write a composition on a topic suggested by Essay 38.

EXERCISE 363: Answer the following questions, which contain words from Essay 38.

1. Would you like to have seafaring as your occupation?
2. Does a sick person sometimes have mysterious desires?
3. Do people usually use recondite words in ordinary conversation?
4. Does a large ship often have to be taken in tow when it docks?

5. Is being laughed at a traumatic experience for some persons?
6. Do you like to be with a person who talks incontinently?
7. Do you have to have lumber to build a wooden house?
8. When you have been in need of money, have you ever found any providentially?
9. Have you ever had a flash of comprehension after you have been working on a difficult problem for a long time?
10. Are you familiar with much of the scientific nomenclature that botanists use for plants?
11. Why should a person crush a cigarette after he has finished smoking?
12. Do officers usually serve themselves in their mess?
13. What induced you to study English?
14. Have you ever seen a tree after lightning has splintered it?
15. Why does a robber try to move around unobtrusively?
16. Is a choleric person easy to get along with?
17. Would rain in the morning be auspicious for a picnic in the afternoon?
18. If a man is often late for work, will he be likely to retain his job?
19. What is timber used for?
20. When you face the front or bow of a ship, which is the port side?
21. Should students be pugnacious with their teachers?
22. How do you feel when you get seasick?
23. Why does a ship need a rudder?
24. When you go to a dentist, does he seem to work on your teeth an unconscionably long time?
25. Can a large fish sunder a fishing line?
26. Which would probably be warmer in a ship—the engine room or the boiler room?
27. Have you ever seen a repairman clamber up a telephone pole?
28. Do young boys frequently decide that they want to go to sea when they grow up?
29. Do people here sit on piers and fish?
30. What do the initials *S.S.* before the name of a ship stand for?
31. Would you be able to have a lot of furniture in a cabin 8 feet long and 4 feet wide?
32. Why do electric motors have plating around them?

33. Do officers and soldiers usually share the same quarters?

34. Do you often see a gang of laborers working on streets in a large city?

35. Which would join a maritime union—a farmer or a sailor?

36. Is it sometimes necessary for a parent to refuse adamantly to allow a child to do something he wants?

37. Why is grease put on the hubs of wheels?

38. Do you suffer from boredom when you are doing something you are interested in?

39. Does a soldier belong to the nautical branch of the armed forces?

40. Are there any steampipes in this room?

41. Are you bound for another class after this one?

42. Are winches used for loading cargo onto a ship?

43. Do fighters take sides in a general brawl?

44. Does a cannon make much of a report?

45. Does a ship stop at a port of call?

46. Where do you find a man-of-war?

47. Would it be painful if a blow of a fist caught you on the side of your head?

48. Do I outweigh you, do you think?

49. Does a mechanic often get begrimed when working on a motor?

50. Does a sailor have to stay aboard ship when he is on shore leave?

51. Can a captain see most of the deck when he is standing on the bridge of his ship?

52. Is a turbine a kind of motor?

53. Can you come to class if you are under arrest?

54. With what material does a carpenter work?

55. Does a cat look bedraggled after a bath?

56. Does a timid person usually have a flamboyant manner of speaking?

57. Would you like to get a haircut from a novice barber?

58. Does an anchor help keep a ship stationary?

59. If you were on a raft in the ocean by yourself, would you be adrift?

60. Would a captain welcome a mutiny?

EXERCISE 364: Write an essay on one of the questions in Exercise 363.

ESSAY 39 BOXING

A stranger at a boxing match will be likely to be amazed at the pandemonium that the [1]_____ cheering audience in the arena can set up, [2]_____ encouragements to their favorite and shouting [3]_____ at his opponent. If the stranger has any appreciation for art, he will be charmed by the [4]_____ movements of some [5]_____ contestants, but if he is squeamish about torture, he may be taken aback by the sight of a punch-drunk fighter [6]_____ on his feet in the ring until he catches a whistling haymaker on his chin and is sent [7]_____ on the canvas. The [8]_____ spectator should be told by his escort that a boxer who is knocked down may rise to fight again but one who is [9]_____ will probably lie there through the count of ten.

Brutal though it may seem, pugilism, like most other sports, has a long history: It was mentioned by Homer and included in the seventh century B.C. in the original Olympic games. After the Romans, who boxed with their fists bound with a knotted, and sometimes metal-weighted, leather cestus, lost the decision and their city to the barbarian challengers, the game died out but was revived in England in the eighteenth century, when pugilists fought with their bare hands. Modern boxing is intimately associated with the Marquis of Queensberry, who introduced a code of rules which prescribed, among other features, the use of boxing gloves, a [10]_____ number of three-minute rounds, the forbidding of gouging and wrestling, and a count of ten before a downed fighter was declared the loser.

EXERCISE 365: For each numbered blank in Essay 39, provide the word or phrase which best completes the meaning of the sentence. Make your selection from the numbered groups, which correspond to the numbered blanks. These lists contain words that appeared in Essay 30.

1.	2.	3.	4.
wildly	reeling	threats	impenitent
perilously	bellowing	anchors	onomastic
biennially	shouldering	hatches	rhythmic

5.	6.	7.	8.
brindle	suspecting	descried	novice
locative	asserting	adrift	crawling
sinewy	staggering	sprawling	begrimed

9.	10.
docked	limited
knocked out	sullen
cut off	piteous

EXERCISE 366: Pronounce the following words, emphasizing the stressed syllable by saying the vowel louder, longer, and higher in pitch than the other vowels.

A. Emphasize the first syllable of these words:

boxing	escort	leather	perilously
stranger	boxer	cestus	reeling
likely	probably	city	bellowing
cheering	brutal	challengers	shouldering
audience	pugilism	England	anchors
favorite	other	pugilists	hatches
shouting	history	modern	rhythmic
movements	mentioned	intimately	brindle
squeamish	Homer	marquis	locative
torture	seventh	Queensberry	sinewy
taken	century	features	staggering
fighter	after	number	sprawling
catches	Romans	minute	novice
whistling	knotted	gouging	crawling
haymaker	sometimes	wrestling	limited
canvas	metal	loser	sullen
spectator	weighted	wildly	piteous

B. Emphasize the second syllable of these words:

amazed	until	revived	biennially
arena	again	associated	impenitent
encouragements	included	prescribed	suspecting

opponent	original	among	asserting
contestants	Olympic	forbidding	descried
about	decision	before	adrift
aback	barbarian	declared	begrimed

C. Emphasize the third syllable of these words:

pandemonium   introduced   onomastic

D. Emphasize the fourth syllable of this word:

appreciation

EXERCISE 367: Read Essay 39 aloud with the blanks filled in.

EXERCISE 368: Be prepared to answer any questions on Essay 39 that the teacher may ask.

EXERCISE 369: Give an oral summary of Essay 39.

EXERCISE 370: Write a summary of Essay 39.

EXERCISE 371: Write the parts of Essay 39 that the teacher dictates.

EXERCISE 372: Write a composition on a topic suggested by Essay 39.

EXERCISE 373: Answer the following questions, which contain words from Essays 38 and 39.

1. Does a sick man sometimes talk wildly?
2. Have you ever heard a fast airplane make a whistling sound as it went by?
3. After you had studied the language for three months, was your English limited?

4. Has ice on the street ever sent you sprawling?
5. Would you rather be knocked out than knocked down?
6. Can you hear a person very well when he bellows at you?
7. Does a professional dancer have to be remarkably rhythmic?
8. Has anyone ever hit you so hard that you staggered?
9. Are you taken aback by something you did not expect?
10. Would you be happy if somebody swung a haymaker at you?
11. Are spies constantly under the threat of death?
12. Is an officer's language likely to be sinewy when he is giving orders to his men?
13. Do children like to send their toys clattering down steps?
14. Would an impenitent person apologize for committing a fault?
15. When does everyone on board have to abandon ship?
16. When a ship is loading cargo, are the hatches removed?
17. Do you think that a small riot might sometimes be referred to as a ruckus?
18. Would you be frightened in a ship that began to make one lurch after another?
19. Would you be comfortable if you lay down in a companion-way?
20. Do you like to be with people who are sullen?
21. Does a young lady usually want to have an escort to a dance?
22. Why does a manager want to look a person over before hiring him?
23. Why are tugs needed in a harbor?
24. If a person's pay is docked, does he get more or less than usual?
25. If you had not eaten for five days, would you be perilously close to starvation?
26. Is it all right for a seaman to go to sleep when he is on watch?
27. What rank does a second mate hold on a ship?
28. Can you descry a person who is a mile away?
29. What country does a Dane come from?
30. How would you probably feel if somebody pointed a revolver at you?
31. Can a boy of sixteen volunteer for service in the army?
32. What happens to a radiator when you cut off the steam?
33. When a person threatens you, does he sometimes use the expression "You'd better"?

34. When you are in a woods, do you sometimes have to shoulder your way through bushes?
35. Do you think you would run if a person began blasting away at you with a gun?
36. Do the Great Lakes in North America virtually make up an inland sea?
37. In which world war was an air force first used?
38. Have you ever traveled on a steamship?
39. Are busses loaded with passengers during rush hours?
40. Do visitors have to get off a ship when it leaves port?
41. Would the captain of a ship be classified as a petty officer?
42. Do you think a scientist would be flattered if you called one of his scientific reports a piece of romanticism?
43. Is an easily excited person likely to make passionate statements?
44. Is a soldier assigned to a group in an army?
45. Have you ever seen the cadets of a military school in their uniforms?
46. Is a general a junior officer?
47. Are you likely to be hungry after a huge meal?
48. Does a portable radio function without electricity?
49. In what country is Kobe?
50. What organization was set up to prevent war through the combined efforts of its members?
51. When do you emerge from this room?
52. Is it a good idea to say uncomplimentary things to strangers?
53. Do you think you could lift the anchor of a steamship by yourself?
54. When does a person pay his train fare—before or after he gets on a train?
55. What kind of person is sometimes put in chains?
56. Would saving a person from drowning be an instance of heroism?
57. Is it dangerous to stay on deck during a storm?
58. Do teachers severely punish you when you make a mistake?
59. Do most elderly men walk very fast?
60. Is it hard for you to recall your own name?

EXERCISE 374: Write an essay on one of the questions in Exercise 373.

ESSAY 40 COSMETICS

No woman wants to be a [1]_____ object. Therefore, as far back as history goes, women have been [2]_____ to apply various preparations to their skin, hair, and eyes to enhance their beauty. At least 6,000 years ago Egyptian females [3]_____ their eyelashes and brows with makeup and dyed their fingers, palms, and feet with henna; it has got so that when an archeologist opens up an ancient tomb, he expects to stumble upon cosmetic jars and applicators. Ladies of classical Greece and imperial Rome, like some of their modern sisters, spent an [4]_____ long time in personal embellishment. Even in the austere Middle Ages, women did not entirely [5]_____ the practice of adorning their person, and they must have [6]_____ a huge sigh of relief when they [7]_____ the Crusaders bringing back rare perfumes and oils from the East. During and following the Renaissance both men and women used cosmetics [8]_____, but another plain period set in during the nineteenth century, when proper ladies [9]_____ refused to be suspected of gilding themselves. The twentieth century is, of course, setting new records in the production and distribution of beauty aids, whose recondite [10]_____, to say nothing of purpose, mere males agree is truly mysterious.

EXERCISE 375: For each numbered blank in Essay 40, provide the word or phrase which best completes the meaning of the sentence. Make your selection from the numbered groups, which correspond to the numbered blanks. These lists contain words that appeared in Essays 36 to 39.

1.	2.	3.	4.
manganese	induced	loaded	integrally
repulsive	clambered	confessed	auspiciously
splintering	lurched	waived	unconscionably

5.	6.	7.	8.
abandon	heaved	reprinted	feudally
vibrate	bound	derived	incontinently
emerge	assigned	sighted	nautically

9.	10.
clinically	rudder
adamantly	cadet
hospitably	nomenclature

EXERCISE 376: Pronounce the following words, emphasizing the stressed syllable by saying the vowel louder, longer, and higher in pitch than the other vowels.

A. Emphasize the first syllable of these words:

woman	ancient	perfumes	manganese
object	stumble	during	splintering
therefore	applicators	following	clambered
history	ladies	Renaissance	loaded
women	classical	period	integrally
various	modern	century	vibrate
beauty	sisters	proper	sighted
thousand	personal	gilding	feudally
females	even	twentieth	nautically
eyelashes	middle	setting	clinically
makeup	ages	records	adamantly
fingers	practice	nothing	hospitably
henna	person	purpose	rudder
opens	bringing	truly	nomenclature

B. Emphasize the second syllable of these words:

cosmetic	austere	production	emerge
apply	entirely	agree	assigned
enhance	adorning	mysterious	reprinted
ago	relief	repulsive	derived
Egyptian	Crusaders	induced	incontinently

expects	another	confessed	cadet
upon	refused	auspiciously	
imperial	suspected	unconscionably	
embellishment	themselves	abandon	

C. Emphasize the third syllable of these words:

preparations   archeologist   distribution

EXERCISE 377: Read Essay 40 aloud with the blanks filled in.

EXERCISE 378: Be prepared to answer any questions on Essay 40 that the teacher may ask.

EXERCISE 379: Give an oral summary of Essay 40.

EXERCISE 380: Write a summary of Essay 40.

EXERCISE 381: Write the parts of Essay 40 that the teacher dictates.

EXERCISE 382: Write a composition on a topic suggested by Essay 40.

EXERCISE 383: Answer the following questions, which contain words from Essays 36 to 40.

1. Do you sometimes heave a sigh of relief when you finish a long job?
2. Can you get a huge piece of steak cheaply these days?
3. How do you feel when you look back at an argument in which you were not kind?
4. Why should you drive cautiously when the road is wet?
5. Is it quite simple to find a job these days?

6. When you wake up in the middle of the night, does it usually take you long to go back to sleep?

7. If you leave San Francisco by steamship, how long will it take you to be in Oriental waters?

8. Are you happy when a piece of information escapes your memory during an examination?

9. Do you understand precisely how a radio functions?

10. Has the weather been unpleasant recently?

11. Do you sometimes do poorly on a test even though you have studied for it?

12. Is it dangerous to go swimming in deep water?

13. What would be a possible explanation for a door shutting suddenly?

14. When is it better to take a photograph—on a brilliant day or on a cloudy one?

15. Do the stars appear a little after sunset?

16. Is today in the early part of this month?

17. Is one of the purposes of a labor union to help its members keep their jobs?

18. When you buy something on an installment plan, do you make a contract?

19. Does the sight of blood make some people sick?

20. Do people here go to school during the summer months?

21. Does it embarrass you when you have to confess to a teacher that you have not studied?

22. How many hours a day are you away from your home?

23. Do you like a person who tries to compel you to do something you do not want to do?

24. Is it easy to awaken a person from a sound sleep?

25. Do you catch a bus to come to school?

26. Do you usually sleep on your back?

27. Does a policeman have the right to order you to do certain things?

28. Do you like a workman who is efficient in his job?

29. Is a sixteen-year-old girl too young to enter college?

30. Have you forgotten all the new words you learned last week?

31. Have you ever heard a window vibrate after a crash of thunder?

32. Do you sometimes change your mind after thinking something over?

33. Do sailors have to agree to serve for a definite length of time when they get aboard a ship?

34. How many men, each weighing 200 pounds, would equal a ton?

35. Why does a student have to learn the terminology of a science that he is studying?

36. Do you wish you were asleep right now?

37. Can a shock from an earthquake be dangerous?

38. What is one of the standard ways to make a question polite in English?

39. Have you ever been hired for a part-time job?

40. Have you ever got a job through a friend?

41. Does someone awaken you every morning?

42. Is the president of a country expected to be prepared to take action in an emergency?

43. Are you somewhat tired at the end of this class?

44. Do you like to spend a day at the seashore?

45. Is the captain of a ship responsible for this crew?

46. What do you feel like doing to your belt after a large meal?

47. Are you grateful when a motorist picks you up on a rainy day?

48. Is Yokohama in Africa?

49. Have you ever been on board a ship?

50. Are you confused when two people speak to you simultaneously?

51. Are you sure of the spelling of every English word you know?

52. Do you know anyone who sings marvelously?

53. Does a person look dignified when he sprawls in his seat?

54. Is there a precise legal definition of murder?

55. Does New York City have a harbor?

56. If someone looking at you opens his mouth, do you expect him to say something?

57. Why does a ship need a radio operator?

58. Do waves sometimes come across the deck of a ship?

59. What are some of the duties of the police?

60. Does a person usually assert something when he is not sure about it?

61. When you were young, did you play a game in which one child hid and other children tried to find him?

62. Does a conscientious man try to fulfill all his obligations?
63. Do you sometimes suspect things that you cannot prove?
64. Is it a good idea to do whatever you feel an urge to do?
65. Does a rainy day sometimes have a discouraging effect on you?
66. What are some of the qualifications that a person has to have to be a physician?
67. Have we completed this class yet?
68. Is a summary supposed to be brief?
69. How long do most movies last?
70. Does the government give medals to heroes?
71. Does an urge for self-improvement impel a person to get an education?
72. Is anybody missing from class today?
73. When are you supposed to come to this class?
74. When do children receive threats from their parents?
75. Is an officer expected to give commands?
76. How do you feel when a friend of yours greets you with no enthusiasm?
77. Would you be alarmed if somebody jumped on your back on a dark street?
78. Do you sometimes feel confused right after you wake up?
79. Will you report back here tomorrow?
80. What have been some of the practical results of the discovery of electricity?
81. Do you know the names of any of your classmates?
82. What are some of the things that brothers and sisters argue about?
83. Would you be happy if a dog got hold of your leg?
84. Is Japan east or west of China?
85. Are you thankful for an opportunity to increase your knowledge?
86. Does a sailor see his shipmates very often during a voyage?
87. What would happen if the water line came up to the bridge of a ship?
88. Do you plan to receive an M.A. degree?
89. Do you suspect that a lot of novels remain unpublished?
90. Is a traveler likely to have more experience than a non-traveler?

91. What is your customary reaction to a witty remark?
92. Should a nursemaid be sincerely fond of children?
93. How many years has it been since the death of George Washington?
94. Do you agree with the quotation from Alexander Pope "A little learning is a dangerous thing"?
95. Does gratitude come as a result of mistreatment?
96. Would a comedian be desirous of establishing a reputation as a wit?
97. Does a baby cry piteously when he is angry?
98. Do you feel uncomfortable when someone stops talking as you approach?
99. Which will make a greater sway in a strong wind—a tree or a building?
100. How old are babies when they begin to crawl?
101. How many times can a revolver shoot?
102. After you have left home in the morning, do you sometimes have to turn around to get something you have forgotten?
103. Is only about half the class here today?
104. Do you sometimes catch a cab when you are in a hurry?
105. What do some men wear stuck in the top outside pocket of their jackets?
106. Is Italy part of the East?
107. Have you had much experience in looking after babies?
108. Does the moon appear in the sky periodically?
109. Would you classify a mosquito as a dangerous animal?
110. Do you feel that you have increased your vocabulary enormously?

EXERCISE 384: Write an essay on one of the questions in Exercise 383.